The Sacred Threshold

By the same author

Poetry
Bombed Happiness
The Orchestral Mountain
Marimarusa
A World Alien

Fiction
Fernie Brae
The Blackbird of Ospo

Penguin Book of Scottish Short Stories
(editor)

The Sacred Threshold

A Life of Rainer Maria Rilke

J. F. HENDRY
formerly Professor of Modern Languages
Laurentian University, Ontario, Canada

Carcanet New Press
Manchester

First published in Great Britain 1983 by
Carcanet New Press Ltd
208-212 Corn Exchange Buildings
Manchester M4 3BQ

ISBN 85635 369 8

The publisher acknowledges the financial assistance of the
Arts Council of Great Britain

British Library Cataloguing in Publication Data

Hendry, J. F.
    The sacred threshold.
    1. Rilke, Rainer Maria – Biography
    I. Title
    823′.912   PT2635.I65

Typeset by Anneset, Weston-super-Mare
Printed in England by Short Run Press Ltd, Exeter

When I come to Cumae, I shall kiss the sacred threshold and go on, a restless, poor wanderer.

Rainer Maria Rilke
in a school exercise

Of Rilke it might be said, as E. M. W. Tillyard remarked of Keats: 'I believe we read [him] in some measure because his poetry gives a version of a remarkable personality, of which another version is his life.'

Contents

All quotations in this volume are from the definitive edition *Sämtliche Werke,* published by Rilke Archives in collaboration with Ruth Sieber-Rilke, produced by Ernst Zinn (Insel Verlag, Wiesbaden, 1966).

All translations of the poetry in this book, and of most of the prose, are the work of the author.

I

Divisions on a Ground

East and West do meet, in Prague.

Isolated on the Bohemian Plain, its spacious parks might be in Dyetskoe Selo, near Leningrad, yet the buildings and streets are reminiscent of Paris. Within the city, Gothic and Baroque, Reformation and Counter-Reformation struggle for predominance.

It was in the old city, at 19 Heinrichgasse, that Rainer Maria Rilke was born on 4 December 1875. The house itself is now a bank, so completely has fate removed the traces of the poet. The child was at once baptized, Reñe Karl Wilhelm Johann Josef Maria. Frau Rilke later described his arrival in a letter to her son (17 December 1922):

> On December 3rd the snow was mountains high, but we
> ventured out at five o'clock, visited Grandmama (always kind
> and ready to help) as the 4th was her Name Day, and then
> Papa happily agreed that we should buy a little golden cross for
> our child at Rummel's. Though it was not expected until
> February, it gave us pleasure to have that piece of jewellery at
> home, as the first gift. Towards eight, I suddenly felt so unwell
> that we requested the inevitable Madame to pay her evening-
> call — she came, and settled in — prophesying straight away a
> seven-months child, hastening to enter the world.... at
> midnight — the same time that Our Saviour was born — and
> as it was almost Saturday — you at once became one of
> Mary's children! Consecrated to the gracious Madonna....
> Small and delicate was our sweet little boy, but splendidly
> developed — and as he lay in bed in the forenoon, he received
> the little cross — so Jesus was his first present. Then,
> unfortunately, came all sorts of sorrows, great and small, but
> when I knelt at your cradle my heart was singing, the lovely
> little boy — was our supreme joy.

As though it were not enough that the child should be born

prematurely, in the dead of winter, into such an environment, the house itself was said to be haunted:

> I have told you over and over again of the second floor...
> Noises were often to be heard, and the servants were so
> terrified that they wanted to give notice, and were unable to
> sleep at night... Now on the balcony flat there are only
> offices, but where I am, sometimes the haunting that goes on is
> awful. There is a peculiar double knocking, becoming stronger
> at intervals, as if some man in desperation were waiting to be
> let out.... I would have looked out, but was afraid of the
> vision I knew I would see.

Frau Rilke concluded that during the Revolution someone had been buried alive in the wall and, unable to find relief, his soul haunted the building. Every night she prayed and sprinkled Holy Water over the spot before going to bed. Her son wondered why the Madonna over the door, with her lamp, could not banish these spirits.

Sophie Rilke was excessively careful in her religious observance, and Rilke later complained of her being 'unreal', of 'praying as others drink coffee'. She made him kiss the Cross where the nails were, and taught her son to call God 'Heavenly Papa', Mary 'Heavenly Mama', thus perpetuating family divergences, which assumed cosmic proportions. Rilke felt that her human love was reserved for the Saints, whose pictures hung around the walls, beside one of Vesuvius which he feared would burst into flame.

Phia, as she was known, came of Prague haut-bourgeois stock. Her parents were originally from Alsace, where her father Carl Entz was a merchant, then a Board Member of the Bohemian Savings Bank and Imperial Counsellor. An oil-painting of her mother Caroline as a girl is striking in its resemblance to Rilke: he inherited her large eyes and extravagant mouth. His grandmother lived until she was 99, unwilling 'to let go', as Rilke remarked.

At the time of her marriage in 1873, Phia was elegant and lively, looking forward to life with a dashing officer. Josef Rilke, thirteen years older than his wife, was born in Bohemia and educated in military schools. In 1859, when he was twenty-one, he was Commandant of the Castello of Brescia in Italy, but on the point of receiving his commission he was compelled by throat trouble to resign. He settled down in 1865 to the life of an official on the Prague-Turnau Railway, dreaming of resuming his army career one day.

Instead, as his wife never failed to point out, he became station-master at Bakor, and later an inspector on the Bohemian Railways. Only once did Herr Rilke almost succeed in breaking away from the life he disliked. Rilke recounted the episode in a letter to his daughter (1 March 1924):

> What exciting weeks we went through, when, very late, much too late, I must have been about eight, he tried to exchange his position as official for that of manager of an estate. The Sporksch estate of Kuka was looking for an estate-manager. My father must have had reasons for thinking that he was quite able to carry out these onerous duties, but it was no easy matter to bring forth proof of the ability he claimed. When young, it is true, he had done unpaid work on the estate of Baroness Weissenburg. This fact was now given the greatest prominence, and treated as though it had been the cornerstone of his life. The anticipation and hope in our home was great. Not only were the financial advantages and health considerations to be taken into account in the change, but the large baroque castle of the Sporksch, in Kuka, was empty, and had been assigned to the new manager. Insofar as I understood anything of the obscure affair, I let myself go in my passion for carriage-drives and sledging, high rooms and long white corridors. Naturally, and rightly so, another candidate was preferred, who had more to offer than youthful memories of life in the country, and our life in the provinces faded away, in disillusionment, into the daily round.

This disappointment over her husband's position was intensified by the modest circumstances in which they lived, encouraging Frau Rilke's tendency to dissimulation. When they gave parties at home, for example, the beds had to be pushed together to make room; little René had to sleep behind a black screen with gold birds on it, terrified lest some dancing couple should discover him. Before these parties, he never knew why, he had to fetch ordinary wine from the shop at the corner, which was then served up in bottles with resplendent labels.

Only on René's birthday did his mother become more natural, though no less domineering. The house would be in a flurry of activity. Scarcely awake, Rilke would hear voices exclaiming, 'The cake is not ready yet!' Or someone would come into his room and walk out again, leaving the door open so that he saw everything before he should. He has recorded that he thought only of 'saving the birthday', watching the others, anticipating their mistakes, encouraging them to think that they were successfully coping with everything.

From his earliest years he was trained to behave with proper formality to adults, and his mother taught him three words of French a day: learning Czech would not have been appropriate for the son of a former Austrian officer. Having literary inclinations — she produced a small volume of aphorisms, *Ephemerides,* in 1900 — Frau Rilke fostered her son's attempts at verse, and his drawing. With her assistance he drew a red knight fighting a monster with a crocodile's head and serpent's tail. Other pictures were in a similar strain. A water-colour showed a dying officer supported by his friend, a battle in the background; this was captioned 'His First and Last Fight'. The most curious still exists, of an island, a park, a white castle and a road: exactly the décor of Rilke's play, *The White Princess.*

René's hair was still long, as was a custom of the period, and he played with dolls. Even during the rare birthday parties, when he was allowed to entertain other children, or else play at 'cooking' by himself, his pursuits were inclined to be feminine. As he wrote to his wife (17 October 1908): 'I see it all quite clearly still, the little pots and pans one lifted as if they were hot.' Indeed until he was five, in accordance with the grim pretence that he was not himself but a reincarnation of the daughter lost in infancy, René had to wear girl's clothes, and behave like a girl. He would stand outside the door and knock. When his mother called out, 'Who is it?', he would squeak 'Sophie'. And when he entered, wearing a little housefrock with rolled-up sleeves, he was Mama's little Sophie, whose hair had to be plaited, so she should not be confused with the naughty boy. 'Sophie' had then to report her 'brother's' misdeeds. Though purporting to be the experience of Malte Laurids Brigge, the poet's subsequent alter ego, this is unmistakably René's. Frau Rilke encouraged a dual personality which persisted in Rilke's mind, and was never fully overcome. Later she would ask him what had happened to 'Sophie' and venture the opinion that 'Sophie' must be dead. This Rilke would strenuously deny.

It was his father who finally said, 'These games must be stopped', and 'It is time the boy's hair was cut'. His mother wept. If he could, René said, he would have been a girl for her sake. He enjoyed dressing up and standing before the mirror, until the day he became terrified because the girlish image was more real than he. His father had taken a hand now and then, providing the child with small dumb-bells for exercise, and with lead soldiers. René was given commands, medals were pinned on him, and he was supposed to send in reports. Neither parent, apparently, could resist the temptation to go too far, in their opposing directions. Rilke lived 'between their hope and suspicion, approval and blame', not himself but a consolation for their private disappointments.

The constant parental fussing was such that illness must have seemed the only possible escape to the child, yet that did not always achieve its object. During one of his frequent bouts, he had to learn by heart Schiller's ballads. His mother, who had once seemed 'easy, warm and good', providing emotional security, began to reveal how little she really understood him. Rilke later denounced her to his wife: 'I cannot bring home to her the least thing that is real to me. With her false conception of me, she sees inside me such a hole, such an emptiness, that nothing retains its validity for her. Who can enter a doll's house on which the doors and walls are only painted?' (2 November 1907). His childhood fears were various and powerful. There was a big shape that would not go away, despite his shouts and tears, that even the doctor could not banish. He feared that the button on his nightgown would become larger than his head. In *Malte,* Rilke describes the evening he was playing with his soldiers on the table, when one slipped on to the carpet. Crawling under the table to fetch it, he looked at his own hand, small and pale. Suddenly, through the white wall, thrust a large and bony hand. He could scarcely breathe, being so terrified of this disembodied hand which ferreted about. He did not dare tell anybody what he had seen.

Rilke saw other children only once a year. In thus cultivating a sense of separateness and estrangement, his parents between them created an aloof, almost hostile attitude in René, long before he was packed off to school to make what he could of the outside world.

What living relatives failed to give him, he attempted to gain from the dead. If his self-reliance, tenacious will, and appearance were inherited from the Entzes, his overwhelming sympathy went to the Rilkes, together with a steadily increasing fondness for his father. It was already a source of strength to him to remember that he was descended from a noble family, settled on the land for hundreds of years. Rilke was the last of a long line, that explained his world-weariness. The blood had become thin, the spirit strained to breaking point.

Jaroslav Rilke, Josef's eldest brother whom René revered, decided to investigate his ancestry in 1870. He hoped to establish a connection with the noble Saxon family of Rilke, one of whom had come to Bohemia in 1440, and had been made bailiff at Schloss Braz by Prince Friedrich of Saxony. Jaroslav's own father, Johann Josef, had come from Türmitz bei Aussig, in Bohemia.

The family was descended in fact from an old peasant family at 19 Croft, Turmitz, whose first owner had been a Donath Rilke. He was succeeded by Burgomaster Matges Rilke in 1625, and his eldest son, Michael, inherited the farm and became a butcher. Jaroslav was not discouraged by this apparent lack of aristocratic origin. The Saxon Rilkes' shield and Jaroslav's family seal were alike. Michael's third son, Johann Franziskus, became Burgomaster in 1774. The resemblance in names and crests indicated that the original Franz Rulike might have been the founder of a Bohemian branch of the family.

Hard as he tried, Jaroslav was unable to establish any more precise connection. In 1873 he was awarded the title of Chevalier of Rüliken, and the Iron Crown, for services in the Landtag. He chose a coat-of-arms linking the family with that of Grand Armorial von Siebmacher. This coat-of-arms may be seen today in the hall of armour of the Landhaus at Klagenfurt. Here too was found the chronicle of the famous Christopher Rilke, one of the Saxon family. As Cornet in the company of Freiherr von Pirovano, K.u.R. Heysterschen Regiment, he died on 20 November 1660, fighting against the Turks at Ross zu Zuthmar, Upper Hungary. He was one day to inspire Rilke, who was already avidly imbibing details of his family's history.

It has been established that the Rilkes only dated back to 1735, but the legend of noble origin persisted in the family, and Rilke himself believed it. As late as 1922 we find him writing that his great-grandfather had been 'Herr' in Kamenitz an der Linde.

It was not exactly snobbishness that made Rilke subscribe to this family legend. It was part of a search for kinship which went beyond the immediate past, until it embraced the dead of other families and other places, the Dead as a community, so acute was his eventual sense of isolation.

In his early childhood, René succeeded in making contact with only one person outside the family: Amelia, a little girl whom he met in Friuli when on holiday with his mother. She lived in a large house and used to bring him flowers. Amelia understood his saying that it was strange how a tree or a bird or a cloud could suddenly become the most important thing in the world. When he finally had to leave her, he gave her a ring. It was a very fragile link with the external world.

II

Dress Rehearsals

In 1882 Rilke began his two years at the Piarist School in Prague. His mother's dominance was still evident in this choice of a religious establishment although in 1884 she finally separated from Josef Rilke and went to live in Vienna with her lover. There was no general plan for Rilke's education, and he missed hundreds of lessons through illness. He looked back on childhood as the period of 'great fever'.

Despite being escorted to and from school, Rilke was for the first time in contact with a swarm of other, alien lives. Laboriously he learned the rules of class indoors, and the rules of play outdoors, but it always cost him a disproportionate amount of effort to behave like his peers. They confronted his gaucheness with 'laughter and superiority'.

He spent the summer of 1883 in the country, at Burgstein, where he wrote to his father on 6 August: 'I eat like a wolf and sleep like a sack. I am a Major of the 2nd Cavalry Company, have a sword inlaid with gold, and am Knight of the Grand Cross of White Iron.' It was a touching presentation of himself as basically military-minded. He was bronzed, had spent his time climbing trees and playing soldiers, as well as playing with girls. On his return home he even drove the carriage from the station. He was unaware that the unhappiest days of his life were close upon him.

Herr Rilke now insisted that his son should go to the Kadettenschule at Sankt-Pölten: it was his most cherished ambition, to which Rilke was reconciled. When he arrived, however, he had to strip and put on school uniform; the cross he had worn since birth was confiscated. After this first shock there was the physical discipline: rising at 4 a.m. to march, swim, fence, and do gymnastics. While Rilke could withstand that strain, the psychological effects were devastating. He soon became known as 'der Narr' (the Fool) because of his brief clowning attempts to escape the strict routine.

The conflicts of this life were intensified by their symbolic importance: a choice between his father's and mother's worlds. If he were successful, Herr Rilke would see it as proof of his own ability, confirmation that he had been simply a victim of misfortune. Herr Rilke warned his wife not to overwhelm René with extravagant letters, or to encourage him to write poetry. Phia meanwhile spoke of the 'imprisonment of her poor child', declaring that he was no more suited to a career in the Imperial Army than his father.

Had he been prepared to compromise, as at home, Rilke might have gone his way unnoticed; as it was, he rebelled against institutional life, taking refuge in fantasy. His boyhood poetry survives in a black notebook dating from 1888, the titles are self-explanatory: 'The Grave', 'Resignation', 'The Cemetery'. A minor success at school would produce a flash of assertion: 'The Battle' or 'Marching Out'.

The most revealing documents concerning this period are the short stories of November 1899, 'Pierre Dumont' and 'The Gymnastic Lesson' (*Die Turnstunde*), and a letter written to Major-General Sedlakowitz on 9 December 1920. The General, retired from the Military Academy, had harmlessly inquired whether the famous poet and a former pupil were identical. Rilke's response was an out-pouring of pent-up feeling and a revenge on that time. For decades, he said, he had denied and suppressed all memories of his five years of military education, which represented a 'violent punishment of childhood'. He had been exhausted, and 'physically and mentally abused, at sixteen years of age, confronting the tremendous tasks of life, cheated of the power of innocence'. It had all come back to him on reading Dostoievsky's *Memoirs from the House of the Dead,* for Rilke no idle phrase. It was more important, he continued, to become a new person than to reactivate past rancour.

There is something heroic in the efforts Rilke made to grapple with his school terrors in the short stories. 'Pierre Dumont' is clearly autobiographical, about a boy's being returned to school by his mother at the start of another term. We see them killing time until the hour when he must be inside the gates. The boy watches the restaurant clock with tortured fascination, unable to enjoy his cakes, engrossed in calculating exactly how much time he has left. 'We still have an hour, don't we, Mother? An hour is a long time, isn't it?' The relationship is idealized, the mother perfectly receptive yet unable to comfort her son. Finally they stroll towards the school, he tears himself away and pushes through the gate, only to be cut off immediately from the world outside by a hectoring corporal: 'Dumont! You're late!'

Rilke would not admit that these tales had any literary merit. They were mere dissimulations, 'little necessary lies to prove himself, and to maintain the self', embodying an attitude he had outgrown. Nevertheless, they show how hard he tried to fit in with the others. Praised by an officer for his riding, Rilke's native extravagance led him into daydreams while still on horseback. He saw himself as a crack rider, a fearless cavalry officer, and pondered the rival attractions of military and artistic careers. Balancing his father's ambitions against his mother's, he was thrown from his horse.

Recurrent headaches after this incident made further training impossible. Despite repeated illness, he went on to the Higher Military School at Mährisch-Weisskirchen in Moravia. By this time he had acquired the reputation of being psychic. Offended by one boy's treatment of him, Rilke cried, 'Now I know *you* won't go home for the holidays!' Whereupon his assailant slipped and broke a leg. Another boy later asked him to cure a headache, and said he felt better after Rilke's application of hazel leaves to his head. When asked to describe a fellow pupil's home, Rilke was about to plead ignorance but suddenly saw a room in which a young lady in white played the piano, while her mother in a high collar listened. That episode frightened him, he did not welcome such powers. Once in the school infirmary, he saw Amelia of Friuli come to his bedside and throw him the ring he had given her. It saddened and scared Rilke, who thought it must portend her going into a convent. Years later he discovered that it was the time of her death.

Herr Rilke was suspicious of his son's ill-health and instituted inquiries. A boy called Oskar wrote to assure him that René's condition was genuine enough: he looked ill, complained of terrible headaches, had difficulty in staying on his feet. Yet Rilke could still write to his mother that he intended to wear the Emperor's uniform always, and with honour. His visiting card was full of imaginary honours and appointments, such as 'Choir Master' and 'Training Officer'. It seems likely that he was regarded as a bad influence in the school, as he spoke bitterly of Oskar's being forbidden to go around with him, their friendship having been 'dragged in the mud'.

His parents finally gave in and brought Rilke back to Prague, where they decided he should attend a 'gymnasium', a school concentrating on classics. Private tuition enabled him to make up for lost time, and he completed the first six Latin courses in one year. In 1892 Rilke entered the Commercial Academy at Linz. Here his real recovery began, although he was persistently haunted by the idea of re-living his childhood ('Diese Kindheit wäre noch zu leisten'). All the joys of childhood of which he had been cheated must somehow be recovered, the problems he had never faced at school were somehow to be overcome. In certain of his poems, notably the lovely 'Childhood' ('Da rinnt der Schule lange Angst und Zeit'), he transforms this acutely-felt loneliness into something magical. In the world it was not to be so easy.

As a former military cadet, Rilke was accorded a certain prestige by his new colleagues, a fact of which he was swift to take advantage. In public he became a dare-devil to the point of foolhardiness, going out to hunt in snow and ice; in private he was hopelessly sentimental, even sensual. Above his desk he had pictures of 'Clarissa' by Nonnenbruch and 'An Odalisque' by Tito Conti. Before long he was top of his class, and regarded by his headmaster as a 'pillar of the school'. His clothes, carefully selected and expensive, were designed to lend him an external authority to which his school-fellows responded. In short, Rilke was cutting a dash, culminating in his departure from Linz with a governess of doubtful character. This 'great storm of passion' caused him to leave Linz for good. He returned ill to Prague, and consoled himself by reading Goethe's *Elective Affinities,* over which he wept all evening.

His studies had to be given some direction beyond Rilke's own notion of devoting himself to poetry. While he read Goethe's *Wilhelm Meister,* and wrote 'Satan on the Ruins of Rome' and 'Maritana' among other poems, the family debated his future career. Uncle Jaroslav became the first of a series of patrons when he suggested assuming responsibility for the boy's education up to Leaving Certificate standard. He intended taking Rilke into his own legal practice, and was prepared to allow him a handsome two hundred gulden per month. Thus Rilke was enabled to spend the next three years preparing for the university entrance examination, with gratifying results. In 1895 he passed the oral examination with distinction, doing outstandingly well in German, Philosophy and Theological Doctrine.

In this period too he wrote 'The Apostle', a fierce enunciation of the role of the artist as the man Nietzsche envisaged: preaching hatred, renouncing love, ruling over the weak and helpless. The theoretical rejection of love was typically adolescent, in that Rilke was simultaneously writing an alarming number of letters to a young woman, Valerie von David-Rhonfeld. It recurs throughout his life, this 'rejection' of the love for which he craved.

Valerie, or 'Vally', was a distant relation four years older than

Rilke, living in a house in Prague-Weiberg that belonged to Carl Entz. She was Alsatian, but her father's brother was the Czech poet Julius Zeyer. Vally spent most of her time painting or writing short stories; her active interest in art charmed Rilke, as did her frequent appearances in an Empire dress with a shepherd's crook. Subsequent critics have tended to blame either Rilke for his part in this affair, or Vally for not giving him what he needed in terms of imaginative inspiration. Both attitudes seem unjustifiable, since Rilke himself later admitted that he was probably insincere, and Vally was clearly too young to cope with his demands.

Nevertheless, for a while they were perfect foils for one another. She called him 'Hidigeigei', her little grey cat, and he called her 'Piepmatz'. 'I took him out of pity,' she said, when she later described Rilke as neurotic, but she also alleged that he 'cost me my happiness'. Her practical help included providing the money to print his book *Life and Songs: Sketches and Leaves from a Diary* (1894), which was accepted by the Strassburg firm of Kattentidt on condition that the author defrayed the expenses. Rilke remarked of the volume: 'External circumstances are to blame for the fact that I was unable at that time to be either sincere or real.'

The following year, feeling that Vally was merely playing with him, Rilke asked to be released from the relationship. She immediately agreed, and his farewell letter is rather shamefaced:

> Dear Vally:
> Thanks for the present of freedom. You have shown yourself noble and great even at this difficult moment, more so than I. My blessing hovers over your head. You were a bright shooting-star in my life. Farewell! If you ever need a friend, you have but to turn to
>
> Rainer Maria Rilke

There was to be a succession of such 'stars' in his life, indeed the word becomes something of a cliché in his letters. Feminine stimulus was a necessity.

Rilke was unsettled and unsure of himself. His benevolent uncle had died of a stroke in 1892, he was estranged from his father after the failure of military ambitions and the Linz episode, and he now lived unhappily with a maiden aunt. With this aunt he went on a cure to Lautschin in Bohemia. Rilke went boldly to the castle there, introduced himself and was received by Prince Thurn und Taxis, who listened to his poems and promised help. Overjoyed, he returned to his aunt only to find that her dog was sick. Between his aunt, who had to have cold compresses, and the dog which had to have warm ones, he was kept frantically busy. Ultimately the dog died, looking up at him as though to say, 'What, you are a man and can't help me?' Rilke never forgot this incident. No further message arrived from the Prince.

While studying at the University of Prague, 1895-6, Rilke wrote and had printed at his own expense *Wild Chicory (Wegwarten)*. The first number, published in January 1896, bore the title 'Songs for the People', and he distributed it to hospitals and municipal libraries. He explained why in his introduction:

> You publish your work in marked editions. Cheap of course. And so you make them less expensive for the rich to acquire. But you do not help the poor. For them, even cheap is too dear. If they have twopence and have to ask themselves — a book or bread? — they will take bread. Nor can you quarrel with them. If you really want your books to be offered to all, give them away! Paracelsus says the wild chicory is reborn every hundred years as a wild creature. The legend will perhaps be proved true in these songs.

The second number, 'Now and in the Hour of Our Withering... Scenes by René Maria Rilke', followed in April. The last appeared in October, with the sub-title 'Modern German Poems'. These volumes contain curiously evocative phrases and compound words, 'Blütenbezwungene Zweige' (blossom-emburgeoned branches) for example, and 'lerchenlüsterner Himmel' (lark-lustrous sky). Although the feelings are shadowy, the concern with possibilities of language is clear. Reading Dehmel, Liliencron and Hofmannsthal helped to free Rilke from his early preoccupation with Heine, the dominant influence on his next collection, *Larenopfer* (1896).

The theme of the volume is Bohemia and Prague, but Rilke declares in one poem that from now on he belongs to the world, not to any country ('In Dubiis'). A character in his subsequent prose work, 'Two Prague Tales', says, 'That must be Czech: it is so sad'; perhaps the minor key recurrent in Rilke's poetry takes its tone from his Slav experience. Though he was never a national poet, either Czech or German, he had many friends among the Czech National Movement, including the poet Zeyer. Rilke also admired Březina and Čapek, and on the establishment of the Republic of Czechoslovakia he went out of his way to send a telegram of good wishes to President Masaryk. He slowly realized however, that like his own Zdenko, 'all his enthusiasms were fragments of a great monologue'.

The Prague of *Larenopfer* is Prague at dusk, more a state of mind than an actual environment, and the first example of Rilke's ability to transform the outer world into an inner one; or as he put it, to render the world of things 'invisible'. The language shows a steadily increasing technical mastery. He was inspired by the Czech song 'Kde Domův Muj' ('Where is my home?'), and this could have fuelled the pride he developed in being homeless.

By this time he had moved to Munich to continue his studies. As an early poem concludes, 'And even if I never reach my Arts degree / I'm still a scholar, as I wished to be'. Rilke abandoned the law and turned to literature, in a state of passionate enthusiasm aroused by his reading of *Niels Lyhne.* Jakob Wassermann recommended this novel by the Dane Jens Peter Jacobsen in 1897, and Rilke went on to read the rest of Jacobsen's works, which he considered a decisive influence on his own. 'For it is to them in the first place that I owe my readiness for uneclectic observation and my resolution to admire, and they have continued to strengthen in me, since I came to love them, my inner conviction that even for what is most delicate and inapprehensible within us nature has sensuous equivalents that must be discoverable,' Rilke wrote in reply to a Viennese bookseller's query in 1908.

1897 also saw the publication of *Crowned with Dreams (Traumgekrönt),* whose atmosphere is reminiscent of Goethe's *Sorrows of Werther.* These are verses dealing with love, dreams and death, refined and romanticised, full of Pre-Raphaelitish emotion, yet conveying a real sense of landscape and nature. A typical Rilkean rhyme scheme, abbba, makes its first appearance. He was 'looking out on the world from a dark cell' and writing dramas with little sense of theatre, but a striking obsession with horror and death. It is as though the iron will which enabled his enormous output impelled Rilke to 'shrink from nothing'.

He spent the winter and summer of 1896-7 as the guest of Frau Julie Weinmann, to whom he dedicated his next collection, *Advent* (1898). Here for the first time Rilke invokes 'sacred solitude', while for the moment he was avoiding that. His increasing awareness of the 'inadequacies' of academic instruction tempted him to travel. If we are to judge by the poem 'Advent', Rilke was ambitious to be master of his own destiny, and in this frame of mind he encountered Lou Andreas-Salomé.

III

'Rainer' Emerges

When Lou Andreas-Salomé met Rilke in Munich, in February 1897, she was thirty-six and had been married for ten years. Her father was the Russian General von Salomé, of German-French Huguenot stock, and her mother was German. Their life had been divided between a fine house in St Petersburg and a country house in the vicinity, where Lou had shared her brothers' studies and friends. She always tried to establish an ideal, 'brotherly' relationship with men, but an erotic element inevitably intruded. In 1882 Nietzsche fell in love with her — perhaps his only love-affair — and proposed by proxy to the woman he called 'sharp as an eagle and brave as a lion'. She refused. Under extreme emotional pressure she eventually married Friedrich Carl Andreas, of Persian-English origin and later professor of Iranian and West Asiatic languages at Göttingen. Although Lou knew that she could never feel anything for this man fifteen years her senior, and had told him so, her resistance had driven him to distraction. In her presence, he had once plunged a knife into his breast; she consented to his proposal in order to save him from himself.

Having resisted Nietzsche's tempestuous courtship and intellectual assaults, Lou did not anticipate any trouble from Rilke. She found the poet nervous and shy, yet was attracted by his 'gentle, unapproachable self-mastery'. Rilke thought her the opposite of Vally, mature, maternal, a woman of masculine intellect. He left for Italy shortly after their meeting, visiting Venice and Arco. From Viareggio, not feeling particularly well, he wrote to Lou that it was only through her that he had any link with what was human. Rilke had thought of love as a stifling emotion, with its attendant obligations, but it now became his 'country' and his 'home'.

His feelings found expression in his diary and his 'Christ Visions'. These deal with the tragedy of a man who was believed to be a god, a theme to which Rilke had frequent recourse. To him Christ had not been God, had not desired to be worshipped, only to be emulated.

Humanity, dumbly encamped at the foot of the Cross as in a Brueghel painting, had refused to go any further in the direction of self-development, thus laying the foundations of an heretical Christianity. Rilke's world is therefore that of the Father, rather than that of the Son who intercedes in a world of guilt, responsibility and freedom. If he wanted no intercessor, it was because he rejected the concept of guilt itself, along with its basically sexual origin.

His freedom and desultory reading now allowed Rilke to make progress, yet paradoxically the very lack of system made him feel that there was something he had missed. He complained that he had not grown up amongst 'real people', and was anxious to absorb all that his 'impersonal and hasty schooling' had failed to provide. Rilke even considered undertaking medical studies, surprising Hans Carossa with his obscure desire to become a doctor. He longed to acquire the historian's skill and the archivist's patience, toyed with the idea of writing a monograph on Carpaccio or Leonardo, but felt that he lacked the 'technical virtuosity and experience'. This increased mental activity was doubtless due both to reading Jacobsen and to conversations with Lou Andreas-Salomé. With her and her husband, Rilke spent the summer of 1897 in Wolfratshausen, in the Isartal, sharing a peasant's house and studying Italian Renaissance art. When they left for Berlin, Rilke followed.

In German universities, it was possible to continue studying for a degree in half-a-dozen different towns, so Rilke matriculated at the University of Berlin to major in art history. The city itself he found 'heavy' and the prescribed books a chore, yet his academic inclinations persisted. Ten years later he was still hoping to 'make himself acquainted with the history of art, and other history, and also with the essence of the various philosophical systems, in order to acquire the few simple truths that are there for all'.

Before he departed for Italy again, in April 1898, he and Lou had become happy lovers. He may even have been the father of the child she was carrying, which never came to term. Rilke visited Venice and Arco, and in Florence began his 'Florentine Diary' in the form of a letter to Lou, hoping to impress her. In the end he felt shamed by the way her kindly reception of it reaffirmed her intellectual ascendancy. It opens with a reply to Tolstoy's pamphlet 'What is Art?' by claiming that God is in fact the creation of artists. Every work of art creates space for some kind of power. After many generations, someone would be born carrying everything within him, who would be the greatest space and filled with all power. All creative spirits would be this solitary man's ancestors. Trees, hills, clouds and waves would only be symbols of the realities within him. Here Rilke adumbrates the cosmic order that Lou Andreas-Salomé said he needed. He articulated his theory that art would become a new religion, and prophesied that the spring of the Italian Renaissance would yet lead to a great summer. On a less exultant note, he met Stefan George in Florence, who informed Rilke that he had rushed into print too soon. This was crushing and precipitated Rilke's departure for Viareggio, where he intended to make full use of his Wolfrathausen studies to explore Italian art and history.

Viareggio was a 'great firework', his first proof that the Italian influence was not to be dynamic for him. Northern countries, he wrote to Lou, had awakened his senses to softer and simpler things, so that the bright, undeveloped Italian designs seemed a return to the coloured illustrations of school-books. This period was his real beginning as a poet and a man.

Rilke wrote the 'Mädchenlieder' in Viareggio. These songs are an attempt to portray the state of girlhood in all its unconscious mystery. The girls are compared to myths and May, the sea and spring; they are full of longing, and yet somehow reserved for a fate that will destroy them: 'Make something happen to us, / See how we tremble for life!' ('Mach dass etwas uns geschieht, / Sieh wie wir nach Leben beben!') They are more like wood-nymphs than earthly maidens: 'the solitude of every virgin is a dense and intricate forest of plant-life with a thousand dreams and mysteries, into which man breaks as an intruder.' They are the poet's muses.

It was also in Viareggio that a nightmare from the past came alive. Looking out of the window one evening, Rilke was astonished to see the very landscape he had once drawn at his mother's dictation, the landscape of The White Princess. As he gazed, the figure of a Black Friar appeared in the centre of the scene. Rilke was petrified, seeing the Friar as the incarnation of religion, of the love his mother had given to the saints, even of his own conscience. The terror and love evident in The White Princess, finished in July 1899, are partly born of this experience, and of the apparent threat to Lou Andreas-Salomé's life, which must have seemed a punishment for sacrilege. The play is set in sixteenth-century Italy, in a villa by the sea. Rilke's stage instructions are reminiscent of Strindberg: 'The sea extends into the audience; the breakers are visible in the proscenium'. The White Princess and her sister, Mona Lara, are awaiting the arrival of the Princess's lover for whom, after eleven years of marriage to a violent husband, she has preserved herself inviolate in spirit. (Lou had been married for eleven years and her husband was certainly violent.) She receives a message that he will come at nightfall, and land when she waves her scarf to indicate that it is safe. The sisters converse about dreams, death and love, when a messenger arrives to announce that the plague has broken out, and the Brothers of Mercy are administering the last rites to the dead and dying.

Rilke was strangely attracted by the period of the Black Death. To him it was a time when the world became once again a world within a world, 'invisible'. Having reached a pitch of external life and beauty, it offered a great temptation to Death to 'sweep the board'. Mona Lara pleads with the Princess to devote herself to her stricken people, which she agrees to do if she can spend one night with her lover. Going to the window to signal, she notices the Brothers of Mercy whispering in the background, just as she hears the oars of her lover's boat. Sheer terror prevents her from waving the scarf, the boat passes, and the figures creep closer. The Princess can only wave farewell to her Tristan. There is a strong sense of guilt and fear, and the implication that the loss of virginity is accompanied by horror, if not death.

1898-9 was a particularly prolific year for Rilke. The first collection to receive his mature approval, *In My Own Honour (Mir zur Feier)*, appeared in 1899, signed 'Rainer Maria Rilke'. Geneviève Bianquis places him in the Austrian orbit of the 'Jung-Wien' movement, launched in 1890. It was a lyrical and aristocratic campaign against Berlin naturalism, inspired not by Heine or Hölderlin, Goethe or Novalis, but by D'Annunzio, Baudelaire, Verlaine, the French Parnassians and Symbolists. Rilke, instead of succumbing to the influence of Hugo von Hofmannsthal, acquired something of the sensitive analytic power of Jacobsen, of the mystical symbolism of Maeterlinck, of the hallucinatory power of Dostoievsky, of the evangelical humanism of Tolstoy, and the terror of Poe. Bianquis concludes that in Rilke's work Austrian poetry achieves European stature.

Mir zur Feier, later incorporated into *Early Poems (Frühe Gedichte),* is the first volume in which youthful conflict is stilled, romanticism becomes far less conventional, and the immense solitude of things appears in all its intense reality. Childhood features largely, perhaps because solitude is most alive there. For Rilke it was a state identical with art, a state of not knowing the world exists and unconsciously creating another, and 'never reaching the seventh day'. The book is permeated with a sense of space and solitariness, especially the lovely poem 'Suburb': 'There where the last cottages stand...' ('Das ist dort wo die letzten Hütten sind...'). It marks the beginning of the development of Rilke's poetic personality: an 'I' singularly capable of penetrating to the very nature of things, gifted with empathy. According to his friend Frau Kippenberg, the compromise between the 'I' and the world is its fate; certainly Rilke's 'I' was consciously 'asserting itself against the world'.

As if to give scope and definition to this newly emergent personality, he wrote *Ewald Tragy,* a novel whose characters derive from the Wolfrathausen period, and whose protagonist is a timid yet ambitious young man. And in the heat of inspiration, Rilke went on to produce *The Lay of the Love and Death of Cornet Christopher Rilke.*

One night in 1899, while sifting through some family documents belonging to his Uncle Jaroslav, Rilke had come across a paper copied from a register in the Dresden Archives, concerning Otto von Rilke's inheritance of his brother Christopher's estate, the latter having been killed in battle in Hungary.

> I was in a country house then and could not sleep. It was a night just like this. A rather stormy night, with bright moonlight. Long, streaky clouds, like dark ribbons, passed swiftly before the face of the moon. I stood at the window and watched them chasing each other, and their swift rhythm inspired the first words of the poem, which I whispered to myself almost unconsciously: 'Reiten, reiten, immer reiten'. And I wrote all night. In the morning the *Cornet* was ready, I was happy, proud as a peacock, convinced that this *Cornet* would make me famous.

'Riding, riding, forever riding.' The ballad, composed of twenty-seven short sections, is musical in its orchestration of themes, heroic, martial, amorous. The eighteen-year-old Cornet is befriended by a marquis as they ride together, who gives the boy a rose petal as a talisman. At last they arrive at a castle, after days of camping out, and amidst the revelry the Cornet gazes at the women, who build 'hours out of silvery conversations'. He wants to cease being a soldier to learn what women are, 'what sort of hands they have, how they laugh when blond boys bring them fruit in bowls'. His dreams are realised when he encounters a woman, and the description of their night of love is perhaps the best thing in the poem:

> They grope like blind people and find each other like a door. Almost like children afraid of the dark, they press to each other. And yet they are not afraid. There is nothing against them. No yesterday, no tomorrow, for time has fallen. They blossom from its ruins.
> He does not ask: 'Your husband?'
> She does not ask: 'Your name?'
> They have found each other, to be to each other a new generation. They will give each other a hundred names, and take them all back again as one takes off earrings.

> Sie tasten vor sich her wie Blinde und finden den Andern wie eine Tür. Fast wie Kinder, die sich vor der Nacht ängstigen, drängen sie sich ineinander ein. Und doch furchten sie sich nicht. Da ist nichts, was gegen sie wäre: kein Gestern, kein Morgen; denn die Zeit ist eingestürzt. Und sie blühen aus ihren Trümmern.
> Er fragt nicht: 'Dein Gemahl?'
> Sie fragt nicht: 'Dein Namen?'
> Sie haben sich ja gefunden, um einander ein neues Geschlecht zu sein. Sie werden sich hundert neue Namen geben und einander alle wieder abnehmen, leise, wie man einen Ohrring abnimmt.

In the middle of the night the alarm sounds. The enemy is at the gate. The Cornet rides out to rally the company round his burning flag, and the sixteen sabres that strike him down, gleaming, are to him 'a festival. A laughing display of fountains'.

On its first publication the *Cornet* did not sell well, but as the first volume of the Insel Library in 1912 it met with instant success, and had sold over 180,000 copies by the end of World War I. It became a kind of cult poem, though Rilke dismissed it in 1924 as 'the improvisation of a single autumn night', 'an intolerable mixture of verse and prose'.

This romantic scrap of his family history was a mere diversion from Rilke's consuming interest in the closing years of the century. He had realised that his interests were too diverse and that it was necessary to make a choice: he selected Russian. On his twenty-fourth birthday he declared that he was hoping for a quiet position as a Russian translator, but more excitingly, he was planning a trip to Russia with Lou Andreas-Salomé.

IV

'Russia was Reality'

In April 1899 Rilke, Lou and her husband left for Moscow. They spent a week in the city, meeting Prince Troubetskoy and Leonid Pasternak (father of Boris), who provided an introduction to Tolstoy. In May they went on to St Petersburg for a six-week visit, and at once went to see Repin, the famous painter. Russia was teaching the young poet many things, not least a social confidence that he might never have gained without Lou. To someone as impractical as Rilke, this was to prove almost as important as his appreciation of fair women, or Russian piety.

Lou stayed with her parents, while Rilke put up at an hotel, from which he wrote to Frau Frieda von Bülow in May:

> I feel my stay in Russia to be a peculiar rounding-off of that spring in Florence.... Florence now appears to me as a kind of preparation and foretaste of Moscow, and I am grateful to have been allowed to see Fra Angelico before the beggars and prayers to the Iberian Madonna, who all create their God with the same kneeling strength, over and over again, presenting him with their sorrow and their joy... raise him in the morning with their eyelids, and let him go at night, when the exhaustion of their prayers snaps like rosaries.

After Pushkin's anniversary celebrations, the party returned to Moscow towards Easter. The season reminded him of Christmas at home under his father's benign influence: there had once been a bell in the room with the tree, a bell Rilke had heard from his bedroom as he now heard it in Moscow. Was Easter so touching in Russia because it was the festival of resurrection, in a land that had lain so long under ice, in polar solitude? He referred to this great experience in a letter to Lou Andreas-Salomé, written in late March 1904 from Rome:

> For me there was one Easter; that was away back in that long, unfamiliar, uncommon, excited night, when all the people

pressed forward and Ivan Velikij struck me in the darkness,
stroke on stroke. That was my Easter, and I think it is
sufficient for a whole life; with strange largeness the message
was given to me in that Moscow night, given me in my blood
and in my heart. I know it now: *Christos voskres!*

Russia was reality and at the same time the deep, daily
insight, that reality is something distant, coming infinitely
slowly to those who have patience. Russia, the country where
people are lonely people, each with a world in himself, each
full of darkness like a mountain, each deep in his humility,
without fear of humiliating himself, and therefore pious. People
full of distance, uncertainty and hope: people becoming
something.

They visited Tolstoy, who received them gravely over a silver
samovar. Rilke noticed the very short legs of the chair by Tolstoy's
desk; Lou explained that he was short-sighted and had sawn them off.
Although Rilke did not understand very much of the conversation until
they spoke French, he commented to Lou afterwards, 'He is great! And
you are right, Lou, he is an artist against his will and very, very
strange!'

On 1 July Rilke was back in Schmargendorf, but in August he spent
a few weeks in Meiningen as the guest of Frau von Bülow, to whom he
had written assiduously. There he studied with Lou Andreas-Salomé,
reading the Russian critics and some Russian history, beginning on
Turgenev and Lermontov. He wrote to Frau Rilke from
Schmargendorf in December 1899: 'I am enrolled in the Russian
Faculty at the University here, and would like to attend the lectures
regularly until my next journey. Every day I read Russian texts for
two or three hours, and books on Russia for three or four hours.' By
February 1900 he had begun to read the epic *The Tale of Igor's Campaign*,
and a diary entry for 7 April notes: 'I am now reading *War and Peace*.
Am at vol.I and fully in sympathy with Prince Andrei.'

Rilke's second Russian trip took place in the summer of 1900, this
time alone with Lou. By now he was almost unable to be parted from
her, and indeed throughout his life she refreshed and encouraged him.
She radiated harmony and security. When Lou was obliged to visit her
brother, Rilke became depressed and found St Petersburg a 'heavy,
almost hostile' city in her absence.

In a library in St Petersburg Rilke found Zabelin's book on the household customs of the Tsars in the sixteenth and seventeenth centuries. He made notes on the furniture, the tame birds and squirrels and their food, on the ancient insignia such as crowns, rings, and weapons, which later figure in *The Picture Book (Das Buch der Bilder)*. To him they were not merely symbols but things existing in their own right. As he wrote during his first visit:

> In fact all things are there in order that they may in some sort become images for us. And they do not suffer thereby, for while they express us ever more clearly, our soul broods in the same measure over them. And I feel during these days that *Russian* things will give me the names for those most terrible pieties of my being, which, ever since childhood, have been longing to enter my art.

Visiting the Tretiakov Gallery they saw paintings by Repin, Serov, Benois, Kramskoy, Federov and Vassiliev. Rilke resolved to write a monograph on the last three, and to translate Benois' history of art. He intended to purchase a complete set of Gogol, whose work greatly impressed him. Intoxicated by such plans, Rilke meant to look for a position in Russia and settle down there, especially as he had already started to write poems in Russian. That he did not do so was probably due to Lou Andreas-Salomé. His subsequent explanation, that he feared he would 'become submerged' by the country, was possibly the conclusion she had reached.

On 27 May he wrote to Frau Rilke:

> Of myself I can only say that my two eyes are scarcely enough. I am going soon to the famous old Sergei Monastery, one of the four in Russia. Founded by St. Sergius, it contains twenty churches and cathedrals and is a town in itself, surrounded by walled fortifications which made possible its defence during the Polish invasion. These monasteries, or Lavra, are visited by all pilgrims.

They travelled south on 31 May, over the enormous expanses of the Ukrainian Plain where, at intervals of days, scattered hamlets appeared like strange outcrops amidst the trackless grassland. Rilke found what he felt to be God in the poorest man, animal or thing. For the first time he felt that he 'belonged', and that he could understand even the peasants, for whom nothing existed between their brothers and God.

They reached Tula, and from there went to Tolstoy's home at

Yasnaya Polyana. Rilke held the Russian in profound veneration, 'the first human being in the new country, and the most touching man, the eternal Russian'. It was something of a shock to find on arrival that not only did Tolstoy not remember them from the previous year, but that their introduction seemed to mean nothing to him; he simply announced that he was on the point of going out. He seemed to Rilke more bent, whiter, smaller, as though detached from his own body.

Lou and Rilke stood about for a while talking, then Countess Tolstoy appeared, to say that her husband was seeing nobody that day. On being informed that they had just encountered him, she arranged a few books and withdrew. Her son appeared later and engaged the couple in conversation. Finally, after Tolstoy's return, and following arguments behind locked doors which resulted in tears and up-braidings, he again emerged and said that he was going for a walk: they could either have lunch with the others or accompany him. They went with him.

Tolstoy strode along like a prophet, his hair streaming in the wind. Rilke wrote in his diary for 30 October that Tolstoy had 'made a dragon out of life so as to be the hero who fought it'. Nevertheless, he was profoundly influenced by what Tolstoy said, by his detestation of mechanical techniques, and by his fulminations against the modern Babylon.

After this they went on to Kiev, where Rilke was fascinated by the Sergei Monastery with its golden domes, and by the Pecherskaya with its incredible warren of caves. These contained the bodies of holy men in barred cells, preserved after centuries of burial because of the chemical composition of the soil. Taking a candle, Rilke walked through the caverns with bowed head, gazing at the still forms surrounded by flowers.

Next they sailed down the Dnieper to Kremenchug, visited Poltava, rode eastward to the Volga, and by steamers made their way to Samara, Kazan, Nijni Novgorod and Yaroslavl. They stayed in the village of Kresta, which they hated to leave, spending four days in a peasant hut virtually on top of the poultry and cattle.

On 6 July they returned to Moscow for a fortnight's rest, before going to Nizovka on the Volga to visit the village poet Spiridon Drojin, whom a mutual friend had cajoled into having them to stay. Drojin had informed the local landlord, Nicolai Tolstoy, who entirely refurbished the poet's house to make it fit for foreign visitors. He was astonished, and scarcely approving, to find Rilke and Lou walking barefoot in the dew on the first morning, but showed them where to find flowers and rare mushrooms. On the fourth day Drojin took them to Tolstoy's country house, where they were so warmly welcomed that they all stayed on, enjoying the beauties of the park and the entertaining reminiscences of their host's mother. Rilke was charmed by Nicolai Tolstoy, who was something of a painter and interested in literature; he read Tolstoy 'Spielmann' — 'I was a child and dreamed...' — and was pleased by its reception.

The Russian journey ended in St Petersburg, from which Rilke was reluctant to depart. Russia's immensity seemed to him a projection of his previous European environment on an infinite scale, and its mysticism a similar expansion of his own being. Writing of the country's future to Lou Andreas-Salomé in 1903, Rilke suggested:

> ... perhaps the Russian is so made as to let human history go
> by him, in order, later, to fall into the harmony of things with
> his singing heart. He has only to endure, to hold out, and, like
> the violinist to whom no signal has yet been given, to sit in the
> orchestra carefully holding his instrument, so that nothing may
> happen to it.

This patient endurance — 'which the German's self-important preoccupation with the unimportant calls laziness' — was one of the qualities that most drew Rilke to Russia. Lou describes him on this second voyage as 'torn between the longing to kneel before each of his impressions, and the opposite urge not to miss what went on creatively within him. Thus he often found himself as if transfixed at the appropriate place of listening silence, and at the same time as if restless at the windows of an express train'.

On his return to Berlin in October, Rilke moved into a small house of his own at Schmargendorf. He had always remained aloof from the bohemian circles that centred on the Free Theatre at the Hotel Saxonia or the Club for Writers, and he now felt an outsider in Europe in general, a 'superfluous man'. There was some consolation in the familiar woodlands to be seen from his window, and Rilke spent days walking there, days vital to the composition of the first two parts of *The Book of Hours (Das Stunden-Buch)*. He grew a beard, wore a Russian blouse, built a 'God's Corner' in his house in the Russian manner, and according to Korfiz Holm, began to speak broken German.

Holm negotiated with Rilke for a translation of Chekhov's *Seagull,* to be published by the Langen-Verlag, but the poet's original enthusiasm was undermined when he found that the play was considered too 'experimental' to be assured of success on the Berlin stage. He was encouraged, however, by his Russian correspondents' praise of his progress with the language, and went on to translate Dostoievsky's *Poor Folk* and *The Tale of Igor's Campaign*. Influenced by the 'byliny', Russian epics sung by wandering minstrels, Rilke tried his hand at translating those, with some success, as well as writing a few of his own. Of his short poems in Russian, six came to him in the course of ten days. They are evidence of the extent to which Rilke had identified himself with Russian life; one runs roughly as follows:

Song

I walk and walk and still around me
Is your homeland, the windy distance.
I walk and walk and have forgotten
I ever knew another country;
How far from me now are the days
By the southern sea and the sweet
Nights of May! There all is emptiness
And merriment, and here:
God darkens — the people, suffering,
Have come to him and adopted him like a brother.

And in 'The Face', as in the German poem at the end of Rilke's diary, the peasant becomes a picture of God himself:

Had I been born a simple peasant
I would have lived with a great, broad face.
My features would have allowed the approach
Of nothing I could not think or say.
Only my hands would have filled with
My love and with my patience.
By day they would have plunged in work:
At night they would have folded prayers.
No one would have known who I was.
I would have grown old and my head
Would have sunk on my breast as if on a stream, . . .
But on my face my grandchildren will know all
That I was — and yet not me.

On these features the joys and sorrows
Are greater and stronger than I;
Such is the eternal face of labour.

Lou Andreas-Salomé warned him that he must work and go on
working, and think of nothing but that, quite independently of her.
Though they still saw each other almost every day, she was carefully
dissolving the old intimacy. Among notes on her psychoanalytical
reading taken in 1911, Lou designated Rilke as typically psycho-
neurotic because of his fear of returned love. When the poet developed
an interest in Spinoza, and particularly in his idea that the good man
loves God but will not expect God to love him in return, Lou felt he
distorted it into doing without the actual *object* of love. In his later
letters Rilke acknowledges this inability to love properly as a cardinal
weakness. The date of their parting is uncertain, probably it took place
in late January 1901. They agreed to destroy each other's letters,
though Lou kept his nicest ones, and Lou asked Rilke not to write
unless he were in direst need. He left his newly composed 'monk's
songs' in her hands.

Late in 1903, when they had resumed correspondence, Rilke
described to Lou her effect on him:

> I had never before, in my groping hesitancy, felt life so much,
> believed in the present, and recognized the future so much.
> You were the opposite of all doubt and witness to the fact that
> everything you touch, reach and see *exists*. The world lost its
> clouded aspect, the flowing together and dissolving, so typical
> of my first poor verses; things arose, I learned to distinguish
> animals and flowers; slowly and with difficulty I learned how
> simple everything is, and I matured and learned to say simple
> things. All this happened because I was fortunate enough to
> meet you at a time when I was in danger of losing myself in
> formlessness.

Or as he wrote more simply to Marie von Thurn und Taxis (24 May
1924): 'my whole development could not have taken the course it
did ... but for the influence of this extraordinary woman.'

V

The Claims of Solitude

Between the return from Russia, and finding his 'new nest' in Schmargendorf, Rilke spent five weeks in the artists' colony in Worpswede, a small village about twenty miles north of Bremen. He had visited it briefly in December 1898 at the invitation of Heinrich Vogeler, whom he had met in Florence. The colony had been established in 1889 by three art students, and over the next decade they were joined by others who had studied with them at the Düsseldorf Academy of Art. They came together because of their common attitudes to life and art, but lived in separate houses, worked in separate studios, and held to no fixed programme. Freed from a rigid academic curriculum, they could paint the local peasants and countryside. The flat moorland, with its fields and dark oak groves concealing small farms, may have reminded Rilke a little of Russia.

Knowing that Rilke was to arrive, Vogeler thought of cancelling an excursion he had planned.

'I suppose he will be able to look after himself?' Clara Westhoff asked.

'I don't know! He's a strange young man. Very intelligent, but insists on wearing sandals!'

They went, nevertheless, and were confronted on their return with the sight of a young man in sandals and a Russian blouse, an Orthodox cross around his neck, standing on the steps. He had a beard and looked like Prince Myshkin in *The Idiot*. Clara was struck by his incredibly blue eyes, and suppressed any tendency to laugh.

'Do you know what he did?' whispered the housekeeper. 'He went into the village in his shirt, with no shoes on. He's been a laughing stock.' Vogeler assured her that the 'shirt' was a Russian caftan.

'The peasants liked me in Russia. We were free and natural. Here they seem hostile. I wonder why?' asked Rilke.

He noticed Paula Becker, the painter, and her 'brown, observant eyes', before his attention was caught by Clara's hands, those of a sculptress. The 'fair painter' and the 'dark sculptor' were like Botticelli madonnas, with their tired sadness and wide eyes, seeking salvation in fulfillment; in Paula and Clara these figures — 'the centre of the longing of our time', as he later wrote — seemed to come alive.

Rilke became an 'Augenmensch', an eye, which rested particularly on Paula Becker, the only painter of real stature in the colony. Between her and Rilke there developed a relationship whose precise nature has baffled commentators. Paula and Clara were close friends, and Rilke kept company with both, dedicating a poem to his 'soul's sisters', which he sent to Paula. He was not accustomed to wooing, having been the seduced rather than the seducer in his previous relationships. Paula seemed discouragingly unaware of him, perhaps more impressed by Carl Hauptmann, brother of the dramatist Gerhart. She compared the men in a diary entry (3 September 1900):

> Dr Carl Hauptmann is here for a week. He is a great, strong, wrestling soul, who does not weigh his words lightly. High seriousness and much striving after truth are in him. He gives me much food for thought.... Rainer Maria Rilke, on the other hand, has a subtle lyrical talent. He is delicate and sensitive, with small pathetic hands. He reads us his poems, delicate and full of insight. Sweet and pale. The two men could not at bottom understand one another.

And on another occasion: 'Waltzing is almost too beautiful, but not with the mystic.'

In his diary, Rilke was cutting about Hauptmann's contribution to one of Vogeler's regular Sunday parties: 'saws and maxims and verses', unlyrical and unfeeling. Worst of all, he insisted on criticizing Rilke publicly and giving him advice. During the week, Rilke met and talked to the other painters, Mackensen, Overbeck, Modersohn, and on Sunday the group would unite. The young women would arrive in white, their dresses matching the decor; Paula wore an enormous Florentine hat, Clara an Empire-style dress. Rilke read *The White Princess* for their benefit, but his enjoyment was ruined by Hauptmann's theorizing afterwards. When the wine was brought in, Hauptmann asked Rilke for a drinking song and expressed astonishment that he could not produce one. Rilke sat in contemptuous silence, feeling worlds apart from the meaningless gaiety so reminiscent of the parties he had hated as a child. He opened the window and door, which somewhat sobered them all. The women leaned out into the night, and seeing them against the trees restored Rilke's sense of their magic. It was a dream world of white rooms, mirrors, gardens, silver candlesticks, clocks and Muses, into which *The White Princess* fitted wonderfully well.

On the following day he attended another party, at the Overbecks', before which he was delighted to receive a visit from Paula. Rilke showed her his Russian books and pictures. Sitting beside Paula at the party, even Hauptmann could not offend him. Still she kept him sometimes at a distance, while Clara showed an open interest.

One evening he called on Otto Modersohn, then on Paula, who had just finished reading his *Advent*. Rilke felt that they were being drawn irresistibly closer together; at one moment it seemed to him that the very stones spoke. After this meeting he wrote in his diary that they had reached this patch of eternity, and looked at each other in astonishment and fear, standing unknowingly before the door behind which stands God.... The sense of intimacy increased the next day, when Rilke talked to Paula about Tolstoy.

By the following Sunday, Hauptmann had left and Rilke enjoyed himself thoroughly, reading his own poems and excerpts from *Tales of God*. They went from studio to studio in bohemian fashion, and after supper, Rilke told Paula happily that he intended to live in the present and let it transform him, and that he had been wrong to try to live in the past. He even spoke slightingly of his Russian trip. They all went round to Paula's studio to make coffee. Paula and Clara went out to milk the goat in the stable, and came back giggling with a bowl of black milk: 'we all drank of the black milk of the twilight goat, and became strangely wakeful after that mysterious beverage.' The people who had the key to Clara's studio were asleep, so she decided to break in. Someone seized a sculptor's hammer and attacked the lock; the noise was so great that Clara put out her hand to prevent the next blow and received it herself. Rilke was correcting the proofs of *Tales of God* at this period, and the bleeding of God's hand may have originated in this incident. Clara at any rate now received the attention she had been courting: Rilke praised her work and talked to her about Rodin.

In late September they all went to see a Hauptmann play in Bremen. Clara cycled alone, Rilke sat facing Paula in the carriage. She was wearing a lovely Paris hat, 'on which tired dark red roses un-emphatically rested', and Rilke watched her eyes, which he thought were beginning to unfold like the tiny petals of double roses, warm and soft with light. The next day Rilke presented each of the party with roses to be worn or carried, to mark them out in the city crowd. It was from this time that the rose assumed a mystical importance for him, and it was to become a key image in his writing. In his diary he composed the peculiar 'Fragment', a fantasy on a dead girl. Unable to bear the sight of her lifeless features, the protagonist takes two red rose-buds and lays them over her eyes. By nightfall they have blossomed and he holds two great roses, heavy with the life of the girl who had never given herself to him.

Rilke felt happy and creative. He intended to stay at Worpswede throughout autumn and spring, and rented a little house there. Vogeler had done some sketches of the Annunciation and the Nativity that inspired Rilke to write, and led to a vision of splendid angels. The people he met reminded him of Russia, with their country air that caused him no anxiety. Suddenly, after an evening alone with Paula, during which he told her of his ideas of God and of himself as a kind of high priest, who could only communicate with the like-minded, he left. The reasons for his move are obscure. It may have been the result of a summons from Lou Andreas-Salomé, warning him not to be distracted from his work, or of his suspicion that an attachment was forming between Paula and the good-natured but unremarkable Otto Modersohn, or because he felt himself falling in love and feared a commitment. Certainly his agitation confined him to bed for some time. He had given his friends to understand that he had only gone to Berlin to collect his books and so forth, and left a notebook of poems behind with an undated letter to Paula, mentioning his hope of a speedy return.

On October 23 he wrote a pseudo-poetic letter to Clara, recalling the domestic delights of Worpswede:

> Pale Westphalian ham, streaked with white fat, like an evening sky with elongated clouds. The tea standing ready to be drunk: golden-yellow tea in glasses with silver saucers, exhaling a faint perfume ... Large lemons cut into slices sinking like suns into the golden twilight of the tea.

In a way utterly unlike him, before or afterwards, he mentioned that he had sent her a packet of excellent oatmeal which he liked best with butter, and ate every day. To Paula he had despatched the complete works of his beloved Jacobsen.

As has been seen, Rilke did not return then to Worpswede. The pages for his diary from this time are torn out, consistent with the sense of shocked recoil Rilke doubtless felt on hearing the news of Paula's engagement to Modersohn, announced on 28 October. The winter was one of his darkest. In his diary he questioned the good of making any effort if one was only to be humiliated. One became a cowardly flatterer, 'crawling to meet every incident of the day, welcoming it like a visitor awaited for weeks and fussing over it,' then, 'disillusioned, trying to hide one's disappointment'. He 'walked in the company of precious memories'. This absolute reversal of his spirits in the wake of the news from Worpswede seems to indicate the intensity of his feeling for Paula. Although he had written to her from Schmargendorf that his lot was still to wander and wait, he probably regretted the self-protection that prevented his taking the risk of her rejecting him, and more generally lamented her transformation from virginal artist into wife.

Indeed she prepared seriously for her new life, to the extent of going to a cooking school in Berlin for a couple of months in the new year. While there Paula saw Rilke every Sunday, apparently harmonious occasions: he sometimes read his poems, such as 'Annunciation' ('Du bist nicht näher an Gott als wir'), and addressed her letters to Modersohn. Clara in turn addressed Modersohn's to Paula, thus preserving the convention of a discreet correspondence, but came to Berlin herself to visit them both. Lou Andreas-Salomé suspected Clara's motives, and warned Rilke against her, yet sent Rilke a letter on 26 February headed 'last call', severing her ties with him. That may have precipitated a decision Rilke was already mulling over when he wrote to Paula (17 February 1901): 'Life is serious, but full of good. I am happy too. So much lies ahead of me. You will soon hear how much!' In March the poet's engagement to Clara Westhoff was announced, and they married on 29 April 1901.

Rilke in his diary expressed the conviction that a female artist who had and loved a child was just as capable as a mature man of reaching the heights of art. He had not said that to Paula. Clara was a gifted artist in her own right, and Rilke wrote that the purpose of his marriage was to help the 'dear young girl' to an awareness of her greatness and depth of feeling. Lou thought that Rilke had been trapped, and it is likely that Clara was pregnant at the time of the wedding, but Rilke later offered a general defence of his move in terms of finding refuge from unspecified confusions:

For me marriage, which from the ordinary standpoint was a

great imprudence, was a necessity. My world, which has so little connection with mortal life, was in bachelor-quarters abandoned to every wind, unprotected, and required for its development a quiet house of my own beneath the wide skies of solitude.

They settled at Westerwede, near Bremen, making a 'strangely-assorted couple' according to an observer. Rilke typically believed that two could live as cheaply as one, essentially on the small allowance his father continued to give. Herr Rilke worried over their vegetarianism and their clothes, warning them to wear decent travelling costumes on a trip to Marienbad. Both were working: Clara did a bust of her husband, showing considerable insight, and in September Rilke wrote the first version of 'The Book of Pilgrimage' (part II of *The Book of Hours*). On 12 December their daughter Ruth was born.

Clara was not domesticated, and Rilke's ability to earn a living proved slight. Casual reviewing, translating and writing brought in little, and though Clara hoped to earn something from a solo exhibition of her sculpture in Bremen, the prospects were discouraging. Then Herr Rilke wrote to say that he would not be able to pay the allowance after mid-1902. He offered to find his son a post in a bank, so that he could continue to write in his spare time, but this Rilke passionately rejected. Rilke wrote to every contact he could think of, informing them of his plight and asking for work or money. He considered giving a course of lectures, becoming a drama critic, being an assistant in an art gallery or museum, opening an art school with his wife. The only result was a commission for a monograph on the Worpswede painters, which he gratefully accepted. He began to think that he must move from 'all that is dear, to all that is strange'.

To add to the difficulties, there was a rupture with Paula Modersohn-Becker. She had written wistfully in her journal: 'Clara Westhoff has a husband now. I don't seem to fit into her life any longer. I just have to get used to it. I really long to have her still be a part of mine . . .'. The relationship was soured by her apparent attempt to give the Rilkes some help, and in February 1902 Paula wrote to Clare emotionally about the estrangement:

> . . . I know so little about the two of you, but it seems to me that you've laid down so much of your old self, like a cloak spread for your king to step on. . . .
> Is it love demanding this? Think about the *9th Symphony*,

think about Böcklin. Don't these overflowing emotions argue
against your new philosophy? Don't shackle your soul in chains,
even if they be golden chains that ring and chime sweetly.

It was Rilke who wrote in reply, accusing Paula of a lack of love and
understanding of an important phase of Clara's work, which required
solitude; it may have been an indirect complaint about the treatment
he had received from her. His view of marriage was unconventional:

> I hold this to be the highest task of a bond between two
> people: that each should stand guard over the solitude of the
> other. For if it lies in the nature of indifference and of the
> crowd to recognise no solitude, then love and friendship are
> there for the purpose of continually providing the opportunity
> for solitude.

He was beginning to feel the strains of domestic life, thinking that it
distorted scales of values. A passing attachment to living in the present
was replaced by a stress on the importance of yesterday, and on the
morrow that was 'more than eternity'. A friend now procured another
commission for Rilke, to write a monograph on Rodin. It was decided
that he should go to Paris to study Rodin's work at first hand, but
before that he went to stay at Schloss Haseldorf in Holstein, as the
guest of Prince Emil zu Schönaich-Carolath. His host was enthusiastic
about the landscape descriptions of Gustav Frenssen, one of the leading
novelists of the 'heimatkunst' school (regionalists), and Rilke was
impressed by their sense of rootedness while still insisting on the
supremacy of self-transcendence. From Schloss Haseldorf he wrote to
Frau Julie Weinmann, soliciting her patronage for his Paris plans. He
had learnt in Russia that patronage was acceptable, and became
increasingly skilful in eliciting it.

> I need the opportunity to learn and take in things quietly for a
> year or so without being forced to write.... I should like to go
> to Paris in the autumn in order to work in the libraries under
> the guidance of the Vicomte de Vogüe, the Russian critic... I
> am very poor. I do not suffer under poverty because it deprives
> me of nothing essential. But last winter for the first time it
> reared up before me like a spectre for months at a time, and I
> lost sight of myself and of all my cherished ambitions, and the
> light went out of my heart. Will you and your husband make it
> possible for me to develop this year in Paris, in quiet and study,

free of this constant fear? I am not asking to be free from poverty but only from fear, and only for one year.

(25 June 1902)

In August he left for Paris, having corresponded with Rodin about the purpose of his visit; his entire life had been altered, he said, since he knew that Rodin was to be his 'master'. It was true that his life was changing, and it was convenient that Rodin should be the catalyst for his leaving home. There, even the people closest to him were visitors who had outstayed their welcome. In her memoir of Rilke, Lou Andreas-Salomé quotes the letter he later sent her:

> First I thought it would be best for me to have a house some day, a wife, a child, something real in other words and undeniable. Westerwede existed. I built it with my own hands and put everything into it. It was a reality outside of me. I did not feel I had a part in it. I did not notice it was destroying me. And now that the little house and its lovely rooms no longer exist, knowing that there is still in the world a creature who belongs to me, and in some corner of the world, a little daughter whose life is closer to mine than to any other, knowing this certainly gives me some certainty and the experience of many simple and profound things. But it does not help me to find that sense of reality, that harmony, which I seek: to feel, to be, real among real things.

Clara was to join him in Paris, where they intended to live in separate flats, leaving Ruth with her maternal grandmother. It was in fact already a separation. Clara was another 'star' for Rilke, as Lou had been, but the expression was beginning to denote irreconcilable parting.

VI

Essentially Paris

Elegantly dressed, Rilke arrived in Paris on 28 August 1902, to be overwhelmed by his manifold impressions of the turbulent city. It was raining as he drove through the muddy streets to a little hotel in a Montparnasse cul-de-sac, recommended as cheap. The traffic was deafening and chaotic, the buildings looked like prisons. At length he found himself alone in his room, poised on a plush chair of indefinable colour, with a soiled patch where his head might rest. He glanced around at the dejected wash-basin; the faded carpet, still with scraps of paper on it; at the slop-pail, with a stump of apple inside. The table cloth was stained, the roll-top desk would not shut properly, while the window barely opened. What on earth was he doing here? The answer came to him: 'people come here to die'.

He went across the street to telegraph his safe arrival to Clara, then returned to his room. Thousands and thousands of images assailed him. He felt as he had done on his first day at school. Here was a breathtaking phenomenon with which he must enter on a life-and-death struggle; a confusion too great for his senses to comprehend; a potential enemy. Yet when he went out he turned to stare at the passers-by in a way he had never done in Germany, because they had stories in their faces. Their lives, full of expression and purpose, were in their eyes; they dared to live openly in a profusion of feeling for which Rilke was not prepared.

'It was the time when the trees of the town are withered without there having been any autumn, when the glowing streets, expanding in the heat, have no end, and one walks through odours as if they were so many melancholy rooms' (letter to Lou, July 1903). When he passed the Hôtel-Dieu for the first time, Rilke saw an open carriage drive in, with its passenger thrown about like a broken marionette, a large abscess on his long, grey, wrinkled neck. It was a whole building of suffering, under which men lived like tortoises. They lived on nothing, on the dust, soot and dirt, on what dogs let fall from their mouths, on

44

any senselessly broken object that might be sold for some inexplicable purpose.

In the midst of this anonymity of suffering, Rilke could be certain only of the loneliness he hugged like a precious stone. The town gradually changed colour for him, and became the only place whose great hospitality provided a sense of home, the only city which could become a landscape of life and death, 'with the lasting approval of its light and generous sky'.

At night he huddled over his stove, peopling the darkness with the images he had seen during the day: the rags and flowers, paintings and carriages; the sick, the dying, and beggars; the gay cafés and grim hospitals, that held him fascinated, like gaunt Gothic buttresses against disease. They stood behind the trees in every square like webs, long monotonous houses with great gates and small side entrances in high walls; in their windows were pictures of terrible diseases. In a letter to Clara, 31 August, Rilke wrote:

> One feels that in this great town there are regiments of sick, armies of dying, nations of dead! I have never felt that in any town and it is strange that I should feel it in Paris, where the life urge is stronger than elsewhere. The life urge, is that Life? No, Life is something quiet, wide, simple. The life urge is haste and speed. Haste, to have life at once, entire, in an hour. Paris is so full of that and therefore so near death. It is a strange, strange city.

From August to September he resided at 11 rue Toullier. The window faced a high wall outside, which 'cut him off from breathing', and there were twelve more windows 'watching him like eyes'. Already his observations were leading to the first incoherent passages of *Malte Laurids Brigge*. Rilke was obliged to take refuge in the Bibliothèque Nationale, and in a letter of 27 September he described to Clara his evenings after the library closed at five:

> Often I go to the Luxembourg, which also begins to get dark then, defending itself against the darkness with its red flowers. Somewhere a drum starts up, and a red soldier walks through the alleys. People come streaming out; happy, laughing, cheerful people; serious, sad, still people; ... People who have sat for hours, on a distant seat, as if waiting, and who have now had it drummed into them that they have nothing to wait

for; and people who live all day on the benches, eating,
sleeping, reading a paper; all kinds of people, faces and hands,
many hands go by. It is a kind of last judgement.

Finally an invitation came from Rodin. Rilke was thrilled to go to
his studio in the rue de l'Université, although the actual occasion was
not particularly exciting. Rodin walked about, showing him various
sculptures, and would say with a commanding sweep of his arm, 'That
needs a bit more in the way of a curve'. The interview seemed to pass
off satisfactorily, since Rodin invited him to lunch at home the
following day.

Rilke found Madame Rodin thin and anxious-looking, carelessly
dressed, with grey hair and deep, dark eyes. Rodin did not bother to
introduce them, inquiring peremptorily why lunch was not ready.
When the food was brought in, Madame Rodin told Rilke in a hushed
voice, 'Eat up!'. The atmosphere astonished Rilke, but he soon realised
that everything in the house was subservient to Rodin's genius. The
sculptor welcomed the poet graciously enough. To him Rilke was a
friendly part of the scenery, whereas Rilke intended to be more than
that, to learn from Rodin, to be his disciple.

The ease with which inspiration came to the sculptor amazed Rilke,
given his own difficulties in composition. Every morning great blocks
of stone were delivered, around which Rodin would pace, perhaps
selecting one on which to start work. The garden was filled with mute
fragments of his white-hot energy, a Herculaneum of eternal gesture.
'Il faut *toujours* travailler,' he would mutter, as one might to a child.
Rilke behaved for a time rather like a child, doing and saying nothing
that would disturb their association. Then he began to shower Rodin
with testimonies of homage and devotion, as in a letter of 11
September:

> You are the one man in the world, full of balance and strength,
> to develop in harmony with his own work. And if that work,
> so right and so great, has for me become an event of which I
> can speak only in a voice trembling with utter devotion, it also
> represents, as you do yourself, an example offered to my life,
> to my art, to all that there is of purity in my spirit.

Clara arrived in October. They met only on Sundays. Rilke alleged
that this 'aloneness' increased and deepened love, since the lover in that
way allowed the other 'to ripen and become something, to become a

world for himself and others'. It was not Clara's point of view, though she tried to understand it. She could not help longing for her home and family, and would stand in the streets to watch children playing, envying their mothers. Rilke did not seem to notice her unhappiness any more than Rodin noticed his wife's sadness; she did not complain much.

In October Rilke moved to 3 rue de l'Abbé de l'Epée, and remained there until March 1903. Since leaving Worpswede he had written *The Picture Book (Das Buch der Bilder)*, a volume of short stories entitled *The Last (Die Letzten)*, and a play, *Daily Life (Das Tägliche Leben)*. The play was influenced somewhat by Chekhov, and by Gerhart Hauptmann; it was never popular with the German public, who actually hissed it off the Berlin stage in December 1901.

The Picture Book reveals a great increase in emotional and intellectual range over the previous volume, *In My Own Honour,* though there is little difference in the underlying attitude. It contains some of Rilke's loveliest poems, notably 'Autumn' which begins: 'The leaves are falling, falling from afar, / As if in Heaven distant gardens wither' ('Die Blätter fallen, fallen wie von weit, / Als welkten in den Himmeln ferne Gärten'). Here he sees everything as falling, his own hand, the world in space, and yet the whole is in gentle hands. The poet is no longer alone in the universe, but feels himself indissolubly linked with the poor, the blind, the beggars, the sick and the outcast, whose world he interprets with unfailing insight. For them, as for all things, he thinks there is no sustenance but God. In *The Last,* one of the characters reflects:

> A song, a picture you notice, a poem you like — all have their significance and value, the same, I think, for him who first creates it as for him who recreates it. The sculptor creates his statues only for himself: but... he also creates space for his own statue in the world... Art raised man to God.

For Rilke God was now not an external reality, eternal and transcendent, from whom miracles or assistance might be expected, but rather life itself, understood in its absolute sense, its omnipotent totality and fullness. In both the prose and *The Picture Book,* Rilke begins to relinquish the ego in order to express things, people, life and death, living in an inner world. (*Weltinnenraum*). He was at least on the threshold of the real, of which he had written while still at school in a fragment called 'The Wanderer': 'When I come to Cumae, I shall kiss the sacred threshold...'.

When he learnt that Paula Modersohn-Becker was coming to Paris, Rilke wrote to her on 29 January 1903, begging her to make up the differences between them, and to visit him and Clara. He also wrote on her behalf to Rodin, introducing her as the wife of a very distinguished painter. Despite their long conversations in Worpswede, it is doubtful that Rilke had seen any of her work and he did not include her paintings in his monograph *Worpswede* (1903). Paula did see them both, but wrote to her husband on 12 February: 'There is still the same joyless fatality hanging over these two. And their joylessness can be infectious. If they were only a little happier.' In his January letter Rilke had tried to explain why he had felt impelled to break up his home. Clara misunderstood the nature of his evolution, and persisted in seeking him at a certain stage of his development instead of following him into the new kingdom of beauty he was creating. She had 'struggled desperately' to retain what he had outgrown, instead of waiting with confidence the new beauties both could experience. The element of conceit in this letter cannot be condoned, but perhaps may be explained by a desire on Rilke's part to convince Paula of the moral seriousness of his ambitions, on which he had dilated at some length at their last meeting. It is apparent that he was still anxious to impress her.

As he had done before, Rilke felt the need to escape, and in March he left for Italy. He had been oppressed by Paris, and Paula's arrival no doubt added to his general sense of confusion. The sun and sea at Viareggio were much more conducive to work; there Rilke completed the prayers he had begun in Schmargendorf in 1899, continued at Westerwede, and finished with 'The Book of Poverty and Death' (*Das Buch von der Armut und vom Tode*): these comprised the three parts of *The Book of Hours,* whose dedication ran 'Placed in the hands of Lou', which hurt Clara. It was his first great contribution to literature, not published until Christmas 1905.

Rilke moved to Pisa, then Genoa, Dijon and eventually to Oberneuland near Bremen, where he and Clara stayed with her parents in order to see Ruth. He reported to Lou that his little daughter seemed to remember them, calling Clara 'Mother' and himself 'Man' — sometimes 'Good Man' — but his letters were more concerned with attempts to puzzle out his direction and methods as an artist. Rodin's example was paramount, yet how was Rilke to adapt his ways to the verbal medium? In a letter of 8 August 1903, he asked, 'where is the handcraft of my art, its least and deepest place where I could begin to be diligent?' Two days later he was suggesting that it might lie in language itself, 'in a better awareness of its inner life and desires, its development and its past':

> Does it lie in any special study, in the more accurate knowledge of anything?... Or does it lie in a certain well-inherited and well-assimilated culture? (Hofmannsthal would testify to that....) But with me it is different; I am ever at odds with all things inherited, and what I have acquired is so slight; I am almost without culture.... as though I had to return to some inborn knowledge I had left, by a weary road which after many windings only leads back to it again.

Back in Paris, both he and Clara suffered from the heat and left the city earlier than they had planned. Although he had requested a single day's meeting with Lou, she had postponed that by an invitation to resume communication by mail first, and that summer Rilke sent her reams about his sufferings in Paris, past and present. She consoled him by saying that his very accounts represented an artistic triumph over misery, indeed they proved to be the germ of *Malte*. He was delighted by her praise of the monograph on Rodin, published when he was in Italy, replying 'only now is it completed, accredited by reality, erect, and good'. Nevertheless Paris was intolerable. He treated Paula oddly, refusing to sit for her, pleading that he was too busy to see her, providing her with a list of hotels in Brittany when she wanted to join him and Clara on a proposed Belgian trip. She seemed to have a disturbing effect on him, perhaps threatened to open old wounds and confront him with new responsibilities.

In the late autumn Rilke fled to Rome, living first in Via del Campidoglio and then in the lovely summer-house of the Villa Strohl-Fern, where the first part of *Malte Laurids Brigge* was written. The garden dripped like a 'full cloud, ready to shake itself out' over the earth. Anton Kippenberg, Rilke's publisher and one of the miraculous and steadying influences in his life, now began to buy up the various rights in his books, concentrating them in his own hands. This was to prove of great assistance in allowing the poet to travel and make plans, although he was perennially short of money.

The Roman interlude proved very fruitful; Rilke was able to write to Lou on 15 January 1904 that 'for the first time in ages, I feel the tiniest bit free, almost festive'. Rodin had advised Clara to study in Rome, so she was in the neighbourhood; while they did not see each other every day, the couple seemed to benefit from each other's presence. On 12 May Rilke wrote at length to Lou, critical of the Roman spring as too showy and sudden. That too showed the influence of Rodin: he had come to the conclusion that to apply the sculptor's method meant the end to awaiting flashes of inspiration; now each book would have an indeterminate period of gestation. He drew up earnest plans for study, and a more precise list of his own work, of which only the first two items eventuated: to continue with *The Book of Hours,* and *Malte;* to write a novel about the Military Academy; to make an attempt at a play; and to write monographs on Jens Peter Jacobsen, and on the painter Ignacio Zuloaga, who had introduced Rilke to the work of El Greco in Paris.

Meanwhile a well-intentioned friend was making efforts to bring Ruth to Rome, in order that the family should be reunited. This was Ellen Key, the Swedish feminist writer. She had met Lou Andreas-Salomé in 1898, and they maintained a friendship thereafter, mostly by letter. Ellen began her correspondence with Rilke by expressing her admiration for *Tales of God;* they continued to write and he was able to dissuade her from landing him with Ruth. Somewhat to his dismay, Ellen had been giving lectures on his work in Scandinavia, apparently making use of private information that she had gained; as he wrote to Lou on 13 May, 'if any man stood in need of secrecy, that man is I'. Rilke realised however that he had to assent to anything that would enable him to go on with his work, and Ellen's promotion brought him invitations from Sweden that he hastened to accept.

During the sea-crossing to Copenhagen Rilke remained on deck the whole time, arriving exhausted yet *exalté.* He did not intend to miss a thing, and spent the morning walking about the city, delighted to find Rodin's 'Burghers of Calais' in the market-place. On 25 June he sailed to Malmö to be met by Ernst Norlind, the Swedish painter who was staying with Rilke's hostess and could interpret for him. At Borgeby Gård in Skåne, the estate of Fräulein Larsson, he found that the trees and meadows, and the simple furnishings of the great house, reminded him of Oberneuland. His letters to Clara are full of descriptions of the weather and the landscape, and often mention the quantities of good fresh fruit and milk with which he was served. In mid-August Rilke briefly visited Copenhagen, where he felt he was in the world of Jacobsen: 'an unparalleled town, peculiarly difficult to convey,

dissolving in nuances: old and new, lighthearted and secretive . . .'. He
returned to Borgeby Gård, where he had his first meeting with Ellen
Key. Norlind had translated her essays verbally for Rilke, and they had
given him considerable pleasure. She was then fifty-five, with the
idiosyncrasies of a confirmed spinster, but Rilke felt that she had made
something fortunate out of an unfortunate life. He always referred to
her as 'the good Ellen', signed his letters to her 'Your son', and
remained on good terms with her.

The rather isolated life in Sweden, though interspersed with
gatherings at which he talked about and read his work to appreciative
listeners, was a period of recovery. Rilke revised *The White Princess* and
wrote the final version of two extraordinary poems in blank verse,
'Orpheus. Eurydice. Hermes' and 'The Birth of Venus', both included
in *New Poems*. He left to spend Christmas with Clara and Ruth, but did
not know where to turn next, faced with the same problems.

His temporary solution was to spend March and April in a
sanatorium near Dresden, which turned out to be a very fortunate
move. He attracted the attention and sympathy of Countess Luise
Schwerin, an interest he fostered with graceful letters that earned him
an invitation to her country seat, Schloss Friedelhausen, for August. In
the interval he spent nearly a fortnight with Lou, the death of whose
much-loved dog caused him to reflect to Clara: 'And once again I felt
distinctly that one should not draw into one's life those cares and
responsibilities which are not necessary . . .' (22 June 1905). The month
at Schloss Friedelhausen proved that he had 'arrived'. Thanks to the
Countess he was introduced to a whole circle of future friends and
benefactors: her sister Alice Faehndrich, Baroness Rabenau, Countess
Mary Gneisenau, Baron Karl von der Heydt and his wife Elizabeth.
To anyone less serious, life in these people's houses would have
constituted a career in itself, but for Rilke it was merely a means to an
end.

Some months before, he and Clara had sent a joint letter to Rodin
expressing their homage, to which Rodin had replied with a kind note.
After further exchanges, and messages sent through mutual friends,
Rilke wrote from Friedelhausen to see whether Rodin might be in
Paris in September; he was overcome by Rodin's response, an
invitation to stay in his home in Meudon. Because of his own health,
Rilke feared to inconvenience Madame Rodin and planned a visit of
only a few days. He arrived at Meudon on 15 September, and with the
exception of brief lecture tours about Rodin and Christmas in

Worpswede, he remained at the Villa dès Brillants until 12 May 1906. The second phase had begun.

Rilke wrote constantly to Clara, in raptures over the welcome he had been given and the life he was leading, as in a letter of 30 November:

> He received me like a great dog, recognising me again with his exploring eyes, content and still.... He has built several small houses, from the Musée down the garden slope, and everywhere, houses, paths and studio and garden are full of the most marvellous antiques, which mingle with his lovely things as though they were relations, the only ones they possess.... Everything round him is in flower... He is beyond all calculation. He told me the greatest thing anyone can say about my book, which has just been carefully translated; and placed it among his own things, as something important.
>
> This morning at six an unknown voice awoke me, a man's voice, most rich, singing in the garden. I sat up in bed, but saw no one outside.... Later, when I went down to breakfast, Mme Rodin whispered to me happily, 'Monsieur Rodin rose very early today. He went down into the garden. He was there with his dogs and his swans and was singing, singing everywhere, out loud'...

Six weeks passed and Rilke felt that he could scarcely go on living there simply as a guest, so asked what he might do to help. Rodin at first dismissed the idea, then thought of the pile of correspondence to be attended to and asked Rilke to deal with that, reckoning on his spending about two hours a morning over it. For a while thereafter everything went smoothly. Once or twice they had discussions about women, in which Rodin's refrain was simple: 'Il faut avoir une femme'. Rilke accepted this as natural, coming from a Frenchman, but tried to convince Rodin that relationships could exist that were deeper than the merely sexual, between lovers who trusted each other completely and asked nothing of each other. Perhaps it was a rationalization of his own relationship with Paula. Rodin's down-to-earth responses were not what he wanted: 'A woman always wants to be satisfied'; Rilke could not satisfy Clara or Paula, nor even gently disengage himself. He tried to explain to Rodin that over the centuries women had developed a superior form of loving that transcended and transformed its agonies; that although men had the reputation of being masters, they were merely spoiled dilettantes, and since so much in the world had altered, perhaps it was time they turned to being pupils? Rodin was too much of a pragmatist to assent.

Clara was back in Worpswede, where Paula was painting her portrait, 'in a white dress, her head and part of her hand and a red rose. She looks very beautiful and I hope I can capture something of her. Her little girl Ruth plays next to us, . . . I'm happy to be seeing Clara Rilke frequently like this. In spite of everything I still like her the best' (letter to Frau Becker, 26 November 1905). When Rilke joined them at Christmas, he saw the paintings Paula had done following her trip to Paris, and wrote in some astonishment to von der Heydt:

> Worpswede was still the same far distant place with its slow mail carriage — country, and yet a strange contrast, an intensity beyond that which is rural here in Meudon. Most remarkable was to find Modersohn's wife in a completely original stage of her painting, painting ruthlessly and boldly things which are very Worpswede-like and yet which were never seen or painted before. And in this completely original way strangely in affinity with Van Gogh and his direction.   (16 January 1906)

From Meudon on 26 January he wrote to Clara describing a visit to Chartres with Rodin, on a bitter day. The first detail he noticed on the cathedral was 'a slender weatherbeaten angel holding out a sundial', which emerged as the subject of a poem in May or June, 'L'Ange du Méridien'.

> As we neared the cathedral . . . a wind . . . unexpectedly swept round the corner where the angel is and pierced us through and through, mercilessly sharp and cutting. 'Oh,' I said, 'there's a storm coming up.' *'Mais vous ne savez pas,'* said the Master, *'il y a toujours un vent, ce vent-là autour des grandes Cathédrales. Elles sont toujours entourées d'un vent mauvais agité, tourmenté de leur grandeur. C'est l'air qui tombe le long des contreforts, et qui tombe de cette hauteur et erre autour de l'eglise. . . .'* That was roughly how the Master said it, only more succinctly, less elaborate and more Gothic. . . . And in this *'vent errant'* we stood like the damned in comparison with the angel, who holds out his sundial so blissfully towards the sun he always sees. . . .

Despite this bracing start to the New Year, Rilke felt generally harassed. The work for Rodin left him with hardly any time for his own, and he was longing to get back to it: in February he was assembling poems for a second edition of *The Picture Book,* published at the end of 1906. In mid-February Rilke met Paula at the station, with flowers in his hands and money to lend her, in support of her bid for artistic and personal fulfillment. The same month he received news of the death of Countess Luise Schwerin, which took from his life not only a very charming friend but also the sense of protection and belonging she in her circle had conveyed.

A more stunning blow was the death of his father, which occurred while Rilke was on a lecture tour in Prague. Herr Rilke was described in a Prague newspaper on 14 March as 'an extremely affable gentleman', who 'was to be seen in the Graben every day at noon, with that fine white beard of his, strolling up and down in the company of other Prague celebrities'. Each year Herr Rilke's kindness towards his son had increased, and only now did Rilke realise the depth of his own affection. He had still felt a child while his father lived, seeing him as a figure of stability in an uncertain world: it was to his invisible influence that Rilke later ascribed the love and goodness that he encountered in life.

Rilke was warmed by Rodin's welcome when he tiredly returned to Paris: '*Ah, le voilà.* It cannot be written, it cannot be described, but he said it in such a way that it was like open arms.' The same letter to Clara showed that Paula was the first person he had been to see: 'she is courageous and young and, it seems to me, well on her way, alone as she is and without help.' He remarked too on Rodin's solitariness, and the concentration it allowed:

> What a lonely man this old man is, who, sunken in himself, stands like an old tree in autumn, full of sap. He has become profound. . . . Always whatever he looks at and surrounds with looking is for him the only thing, the world, in which everything takes place; if he is modelling a hand, it is alone in space, and there is nothing except a hand; in six days God made only a hand, and poured waters around it and arched the heavens over it; and rested over it when all was completed, and there was glory and a hand.   (2 April 1906)

Clara would occasionally lunch with her husband at the Rodins', where they all might stand up and throw food out the window to the goats and cows in the field. Yet the same constrained atmosphere that

Rilke noticed on his first visit prevailed, obvious to everyone but Rodin, whose heroic self-absorption he had to admire. Once Rilke mentioned how the spring seemed to affect one and make one want to work, and Rodin replied, 'I never pay any attention to these things.' They would sit together for hours in the garden without saying a word, and then Rodin would rise and rub his hands as he returned to the house, saying to the wonder of the poet, 'We *have* done a lot of work this morning!' The man seemed so tireless that Rilke too may have felt like 'a cup held under a waterfall', as he remarked of poor Madame Rodin.

It was from Rodin that he had learnt all that he wanted to put into practice when writing; he chafed to write and could not because of Rodin's demands on his time. The sculptor taught him to concentrate, to prepare patiently, above all to see steadily, so that 'only things talk to me.... They refer me to the prototypes; to the stirring lively world, seen simply and without interpretation as the occasion for things'. The fruits were poems such as those arising from his visits to the Jardin des Plantes, 'The Panther' — earliest of *New Poems* — and 'The Flamingos'. A prose description entitled 'The Lion's Cage' (c.1907), discovered in 1942 and now the property of an Italian diplomat, provides the matrix of another such poem:

She goes up and down like the sentries at the end of the world, where there is nothing more. And there is longing in her, as in the sentries, scraps of longing. There must be mirrors somewhere down in the sea, mirrors from the cabins of sunken ships, parts of mirrors which of course no longer hold anything: no faces of travellers, nor their gestures; nor how they turned round... But as seaweed perhaps, a sinking polyp, the sudden face of a fish or even water itself... call forth resemblances in these mirrors, distant ones, counterfeit ones... so memories, and fragments of memories, lie in the dark in the depths of her blood.

She paces about him, about the lion who is sick. Sickness calls forth no anxiety in him and does not lessen his stature: it merely encloses him. As he lies there, the paws slightly apart and purposeless, the haughty face encircled by the mane, the eyes not at all heavy, he is collected into himself, in memory of his sadness, as once he was the exaggeration of his strength.

Now and then there is a twitch in the muscles and a tension. Here and there, too far apart, little spots of anger form: the blood must surely be leaping evilly from the chambers of the heart, must still possess the cautious, well-tried methods of sudden resolve, when it reaches the brain. But he lets it all happen because it is not yet finished, . . . Only from a distance, as if held far from him, he paints with the soft brush of his tail again and again a small semi-circular shape of indescribable contempt. And this goes on so significantly, that the lioness stops and looks, anxiously, excitedly, expectantly at him.

Then she resumes her pacing up and down, the disconsolate, ridiculous pacing of the sentry forever retracing his own footsteps. She paces and paces, and often her distracted mask appears round and full, marked by the bars. . . .

The harder Rilke worked, the more he felt the strain of life in Meudon; equally he felt it impossible to leave, especially after Rodin had influenza and made only a slow recovery. They seemed to be getting on reasonably well: contrary to his absolute rule, Rodin allowed Rilke to be present at the first sittings of George Bernard Shaw, who came to be sculpted in mid-April. Yet difficulties were not far from the surface, and erupted when Rilke opened a letter from a mutual friend addressed to Rodin, answering it without informing him. A quarrel ensued, at the end of which Rodin showed Rilke the door. He wrote in haste to Clara that evening, not wishing to mention the immediate cause of the rupture: 'I am full of expectation and happy. . . . I bore everything, even these last days, with a quiet inward patience, and I could have borne it for another month or two. But the Master must have felt that I suffered.' Rodin's reaction to a trivial lapse was extreme, even if provoked by Rilke's possibly martyred demeanour over the previous months, and drew from the poet a letter both indignant and dignified. Written from Paris the day after his departure, 12 May 1906, it ultimately preserved their friendship:

> You yourself offered me your friendship; and I accepted it
> timidly, gradually, as I entered upon it, making no other use of
> that priceless preference than to enjoy it in the depths of my
> spirit. . . . If I felt that I had to interpret your intentions, so as
> to be really useful, and to anticipate your decisions, this should
> not be criticized. Instead, I have been dismissed like a thieving

servant, all of a sudden,... I was *not* your secretary, with
whom such a step might have been taken. I am profoundly hurt
by it. But I understand. I understand that the cognitive part of
your existence is obliged to reject at once whatever seems
inimical to it, in order to preserve its own functions intact —
as the eye rejects the foreign body which disturbs its vision....
So, grand Maître, you have become invisible for me, as if you
had ascended into the skies, where you belong. I shall see you
no more. But life begins for me now, as it did for the Apostles
when they were left sad and alone: a life which will celebrate
your high example, and find in you its consolation, its
justification and its strength.

It was this moment that Ellen Key chose to descend on Paris, hoping
for an introduction to Rodin, which Rilke could no longer effect
personally. He was revising the *Cornet* and correcting the second
edition of *The Picture Book,* tasks which he told Clara would prevent
their being together, but he admitted to feeling bound to spend some
time with Ellen. She insisted that he live according to her means,
waiting for buses and snatching meals at dingy restaurants; as much as
he disliked this way of living, Rilke had to concede to Clara, 'it results
in a freedom which you and I could well do with. You can do a whole
lot in this way, and could last out indefinitely' (letter of 29 May). He
accepted that Ellen knew what it was to struggle, and that she could
not afford to play the patroness like others of his acquaintance, but
predictably he hated her gushing over the works of art they saw
together. They said goodbye at Fontainebleau in mid-June, with relief
on Rilke's part and a renewal of his affection. He was anxious,
however, about her plans to publish her essay on his work as a book,
and wrote to implore her not to do so: 'the essay, built up so much on
extracts from letters for which there is as yet no evidence in my books,
outdistances me on the one hand, while on the other it fixes my
religious development at a stage beyond which it has in part already
progressed.' (6 November) It seemed to Rilke that she would never get
beyond *Tales of God* to an understanding of his later work, such as 'The
Book of Poverty and Death'. Despite his entreaties, Ellen published an
essay in 1911, 'Rainer Maria Rilke: A God-Seeker', that made him
extremely uncomfortable.

In 'The Book of Poverty and Death' Rilke sets aside his longing for
the kind of pilgrimage towards God that he felt was possible in the

emptiness of Russia, travelling 'behind some blind elder the road that
no one knows', and finds God in a transmutation of the lives of the poor
and outcast: 'the most deeply destitute, the beggar with the hidden
face' ('Du aber bist der tiefste Mittellose, / der Bettler mit
verborgenem Gesicht'). Out of his acute sense of the miseries, cruelty,
indifference of life in Paris, out of his obsession with the disease,
accidents and routine deaths in the city, Rilke created these poems
with their particular emphasis on the individual's need to 'die his own
death'. The dehumanizing society robbed people not only of everything that made daily life bearable, but also of any dignity in dying: no
facile concept, instead, the culmination of significant living.

> O Lord give everyone his own death,
> the dying that emerges from that life
> where he had love, significance and dearth.
>
> For we are nothing but the bark and leaf.
> The great Death that we all have in ourselves
> is the fruit, round which everything revolves.
>
> O Herr, gib jedem seinen eignen Tod,
> das Sterben, das aus jenem Leben geht,
> darin er Liebe hatte, Sinn und Not.
>
> Denn wir sind nur die Schale und das Blatt.
> Der grosse Tod, den jeder in sich hat,
> das ist die Frucht, um die sich alles dreht.

Thirty-seven new poems were ready for inclusion in the second
edition of *The Picture Book,* showing an increased power of entering
into the mind of his creations, and not merely a power of description.
The discipline this productivity required Rilke described in a letter to
Clara on 29 June:

> Already I am wavering in my absolute determination to shut
> myself up daily, wherever I am and in whatever external
> circumstances, for a certain number of hours for my work's
> sake: I do not know whether it will really come now or
> whether I am just making appropriate but fruitless gestures. . . .
> So will I kneel down and stand up, daily, alone in my room,
> and will hold sacred all that befalls me there: even what has *not*

come, even disappointment, even desertion.

He was restless and needed to get away from Paris in the summer heat, the Rilkes were in dire financial straits, so a trip to Belgium with Clara and Ruth at Karl von der Heydt's expense was providential. It was ten months before Rilke returned to Paris: von der Heydt entertained them at Godesberg, Frau Alice Faehndrich took her sister's place as their hostess at Schloss Friedelhausen. Hints that the late Countess Schwerin would have approved of his going to Greece got Rilke nowhere with Heydt, who preferred him to stay in Germany, so autumn found him unhappily in Berlin with Clara.

It seemed that events — and patrons — were conspiring to keep him from Paris. Had he been there, he might have supported Paula in her resistance to pressure from family and friends, and from Otto Modersohn who had written constantly and was now visiting her, to abandon her independent existence and return home. As it was, he wrote to Ellen Key on 6 November, he snatched at Frau Faehndrich's invitation to stay at her villa on Capri: 'With a heavy heart I gave up the idea of Paris, which was so favourable to my work, but it is indeed a great joy that this other possibility is there, and I hope for a good winter.'

VII

The New Poetry

In late November Rilke travelled to Capri via Naples, where he carried his solitude 'around like a treasure in that gloriously strange world', as he wrote to the von der Heydts. The dominant note in all his correspondence from the island, until the spring and his discovery of Anacapri, was that struck in this early letter: 'Always I grow really melancholy in such beauty-spots as these, faced with this obvious, praise-ridden, incontestable loveliness.... Perhaps we may *begin* with this picture-book kind of beauty, learn to see and love, but I am rather too far advanced to exclaim A and O in front of it' (from the Villa Discopoli, 11 December 1906). It was a period of dissatisfaction, not least with his marriage.

Rilke wanted a human being, in his own words, 'who could reduce the things he had exaggerated to the commonplace and ordinary again', and Clara could not fill that role. Although they had both been invited to Capri, Rilke had prevailed on her to stay behind; a situation entirely familiar to her, since between 1902 and 1910 they had not spent a total of more than three years together, and even then very rarely under the same roof. While Rilke wrote to Ruth, and visited her on the occasions he went to Germany, he did not seem aware of his responsibilities as a father. Clara had fought hard to understand her husband and to save something of her marriage, but she must have felt particularly depressed by their prospects that winter — with their first Christmas apart looming up — and have confided her feelings to Lou Andreas-Salomé. Rilke wrote to Clara on 17 December: 'If Lou only knew how many such letters I write to myself in thought. Long letters full of such objections....'. His letter was lengthy, evasive, defensive, but made his position quite clear: his conception of 'duty' was related only to his art, which could be fostered by an unencumbered existence; 'only on this spot can I be reached by the fate, the encouragement, the powers that want to reach me...'. He asked rhetorically whether they did not still inhabit an invisible 'house of our heart', with the plain implication that a material establishment was beyond his domain, and indeed his desire.

Yet if he was incapable of sustaining a marital relationship, Rilke took a genuine, friendly interest in Clara's progress as an artist. He had continually drawn Rodin's attention to her work, and could not have been more delighted when out of the blue Clara was offered a trip to Egypt, and a commission to execute there. His imagination fed on her letters and sketches, he described the desert and the Sphinx, asking whether they stirred in her a sense of unending space, and if 'the face sent forth images . . . beyond the furthest stars to where no images had ever been' (20 January 1907). Rilke's correspondence was his chief means of communication with a very large circle of friends and readers, vital to his poetry in the way that reviews, essays or lectures are for other poets. If his letters to Lou were more confessional, those to Clara reveal her as his most important correspondent at least until 1910.

As for his work, Rilke complained that he did not have the requisite solitude at the villa, however considerate his hostess, and could produce nothing. In fact, at Frau Faehndrich's request, he had undertaken the translation of *Sonnets from the Portuguese:* 'crystals of feeling, so clear, so right, shiningly mysterious and issuing from some deep, unbewildered place in the poet' (letter to Baroness Uexküll, 15 April). Of the *New Poems* some had their beginning or their final version drafted on Capri, notably 'Alcestis' and 'The Bowl of Roses' ('Die Rosenschale'). He may have been unsettled by the news of Paula's eventual capitulation in the early spring and of her return to Worpswede, where it was announced that she was pregnant. In a letter to her of 17 March, Rilke blamed himself for not having asked her to join them in Belgium the previous summer, and said that he expected great things of her art: 'If external circumstances are different from what we once thought they would be, the main thing is that you should bear them bravely and attain the freedom which, under existing circumstances, is necessary to what you feel within you . . .'.

At the beginning of June, with help from Ellen Key, Rilke was back in Paris. He left Capri without the slightest regret, and despite the old distressing aspects of the city, he could write to Clara: 'Everything is there again, reality down to the smallest particle. You go for a walk and are simply and sheerly happy . . .' (3 June 1907). Rilke settled down to work immediately, sent Clara the manuscript of the first volume of

New Poems by the end of the month, and in July completed his second essay on Rodin. The great event of this period in Paris was the *Salon d'automne,* at which Rilke discovered the work of Cézanne.

It was a revelation. Some of his best letters to Clara are those he wrote describing Cézanne's paintings and recounting the life of a man with whom he felt the deepest affinity. Gaining confidence in the new direction his poetry was taking, Rilke at thirty-two was encouraged by the example of Cézanne's only plunging into work at forty, under Pissarro's influence. He recreated for Clara Cézanne's 'continual rage' that sustained him for thirty years of unremitting work (from 29, rue Cassette, 9 October):

> ... Old, ill, wearied every evening to the point of unconsciousness by the regularity of his daily work ... surly, mistrustful, laughed at, hooted at, treated with contumely every time he went to his studio — but celebrating his Sundays, hearing mass and vespers like a child ... his mother he loved too, but when she was buried he was not there. He happened to be *'sur le motif',* as he called it. Even in those days his work was so important to him and brooked no exception ...
>
> Outside, an indeterminate horror on the increase; a little nearer, indifference and mockery, and then, suddenly, this old man deep in his work, painting nudes only from drawings done forty years ago in Paris, knowing that no model would be allowed him in Aix.... So he paints from his old drawings. And lays his apples on counterpanes, which Madame Brémond is sure to find missing one day, and places his wine-bottles inbetween and anything he can lay hands on. And (like Van Gogh) makes his 'saints' out of such things; forces them, *forces* them to be beautiful, to mean the whole world and all its happiness and splendour, and does not know whether he has really succeeded in making them so. And he sits in the garden like an old dog —

A few days later he reported that he had asked Mathilde Vollmoeller to go to the Salon with him, so that he could compare his impressions with someone he trusted: 'Cézanne did not let us go on to anything else' (12 October). 'But imagine my astonishment,' he continued, 'when Fräulein V., trained and using her eye wholly as a painter, said: "Like a dog he sat in front of it and simply looked, without any nervousness or irrelevant speculation".' This was the essence of

Cézanne's lesson for Rilke, spelt out in the next day's letter to Clara:

... If I came to you I should certainly see the magnificence of moorland and heath, the drifting luminous green of meadows and birches in a new and different way; but although these changes ... did indeed call forth a part of the *Stunden-Buch,* yet in those days Nature was still a sort of general excitation for me, an upsurge of feeling ... I walked alone and saw not Nature but the visions she gave me. How little I should then have known how to learn from Cézanne, from Van Gogh! ... I was with his pictures again today ... one notices, better each time, how necessary it was to get beyond even love; it comes naturally to love each of these things when one makes them; but if one shows this, one makes them less well; one *judges* them instead of *saying* them. One stops being impartial and love, the best thing, remains outside the work, does not enter it, remains untransmuted beside it: this was how impressionist painting arose (which is no better than the realist school). One painted 'I love this' instead of painting 'Here it is'. Whereby everyone is forced to see for himself whether I have loved it. ... This consuming of love in anonymous work, which gives rise to such pure things, probably no one has succeeded in doing so completely as old Cézanne ...

I have received the first proofs [of the *Neue Gedichte*] from the Insel. In the poems there are the instinctive beginnings of a similar objectivity. ...

In a letter of 21 October, Rilke speculated on the relationship between Cézanne's achievement and his inarticulacy on the subject of painting, although his last wish was clear and literally fulfilled:

'Je me suis juré de mourir en peignant.' As in an old picture of the Danse Macabre, Death seized his hand from behind and painted the last stroke himself, trembling with pleasure; long had his shadow been lying across the palette and he had had time to choose, in the open, crescent-like sequence of colours the one that pleased him best; as soon as it got on to the brush he would snatch it up and paint. ...

On the 22nd the Salon closed, but in a few subsequent letters Rilke continued to record tones and details of the paintings. The 23rd was the second anniversary of Cézanne's death; after a description of his *Self*

Portrait, Rilke wrote to Clara: 'perhaps you can glimpse a little of him from all this, the old man characterized by the words he himself laid at the feet of Pissarro: "*humble et colossal*".'

Rilke did not have Cézanne's stamina, however, and was longing for a change of scene. He thus accepted invitations to read his own poetry and lecture on Rodin, leaving for Prague at the beginning of November. He still felt ill at ease in the city, both saddened and threatened by the buildings and the childhood memories they evoked. The sight of four Cézannes cheered him, as did the receipt of a friendly letter from Rodin. The Baroness Nádherný made him welcome at her castle in Breslau, whence he wrote to Clara on 4 November about his reception in Prague:

> Everybody wanted me as though I were something to eat —
> but as soon as they got me I found they weren't hungry and
> had to keep to a diet. My mother untiring in her efforts to do
> everything possible for me — but... The lecture was dreary;
> again the frightful old ladies who used to astonish me as a
> child... not a bit more amusing now that the astonishment is
> on their side....

In Vienna all his disappointments were put into the shade by a letter from Rodin requesting a reconciliation. A jubilant Rilke communicated the close of the letter to Clara (11 November):

> It runs: '*Venez, quand vous êtes à Paris, me voir. Des choses, des
> choses. Nous avons besoin de la vérité, de la poésie tous deux et d'amitié.*'
> How good and just he is, experiencing things so honestly from
> his work! How *just!* I have always known that he was so, and
> you knew it too. He thinks fondly of you.... He was pleased
> with the essay in *Kunst und Künstler: 'votre étude... je la trouve très
> belle de vérité....*'

Later during the tour he heard that Paula had given birth to a daughter on 2 November. He arrived happily enough for a much-desired holiday in Venice, having taken up the offer of rooms in the Palazzo Zatteri from the art historian, Julius Meyer Graefe. The household had been expecting a Frau Maria Rilke, so there was mutual surprise when the poet presented himself. It was there that he learnt of Paula's death of a heart-attack on 21 November.

There is no record of his immediate reaction: subsequent letters are full of complaints of exhaustion and ill-health, and illness finally overtook him in Oberneuland in mid-February, 1908. It was the second time such a prolonged bout of sickness had occurred in the wake of bad news of Paula. Later he confessed to Katherine Kippenberg that she was the only one of his dead friends to trouble him, and surely it is to Paula that Rilke makes veiled reference in a letter to Countess Kanitz-Menar (16 July 1908):

> The death of the Countess Schwerin and the death of my father (both of whom gave me to feel their infinite nobility and greatness of spirit) have caused me to fear this question no longer.... I stand towards death in such a way that it shocks me more in those whom I have neglected, who have remained inexplicable or fateful to me, than in those whom I loved with certainty while they lived...

When Rilke came across an edition of Paula's letters and diaries in December 1923, he wrote to Clara saying that he felt he ought to dedicate the *Duino Elegies* and *Sonnets to Orpheus* to Paula's memory, so that she might forgive him everything. He would not have said such a thing lightly.

As soon as he was able, Rilke started on a restless journey: from Berlin to Rome to Naples to Capri, where he stayed at the Villa Discopoli until mid-April. There were three women in the house: the old Baroness von Nordeck zu Rabenau (Frau Nonna), Frau Faehndrich, and her niece Manon zu Solms-Laubach. In the evenings Rilke liked sitting with them as they sewed or peeled him an apple, gathering his strength. Not the least of the problems he faced was the perennial lack of finance, but he dealt with that by writing an important letter to his publisher on 11 March. He explained to Kippenberg that he intended to return to Paris, to live in the solitude always conducive to his work there. This had been possible in the past through a series of grants, but now that the prospect of a state subsidy had fallen through, he wanted to discover whether his past and future writings could not guarantee him some kind of income. The letter was carefully phrased and Kippenberg's response was apparently generous. He now became Rilke's banker as well as publisher, friend and confidant in family matters, consistently behaving with intelligence and tact.

Rilke returned to Paris in July: on 1 September 1908 he moved into the Hotel Biron, 77 rue de Varenne, now the Musée Rodin. Clara let him use her studio there in her absence, and when she returned he also took rooms in the building. He was pleased by Rodin's coming to see him as soon as he was settled, and gave an account to Clara of their discussions about women and love, which had ended at a familiar impasse. Rilke could now support his contentions by referring to the case of Marianna Alcoforado, the Portuguese nun whose love-letters had been brought to his attention in Capri. The originals of these letters have not been discovered, but Rilke began translating them from the French, and wrote a lyrically enthusiastic account of them for the *Inselalmanach* in 1908. As he wrote later to Fräulein Annette Kolb, the example of the nun, 'this extreme lover and her ignominious partner', served perfectly to demonstrate his conviction that 'whatever there is in love of achievement, of suffering, of consummation is on the one side only, the side of the woman, as contrasted with the utter inadequacy of the man' (23 January 1912). Yet there was no doubt that some women made palpable demands, and in a letter of 4 September he made stern reply to Clara's: 'Please, let me be and have trust in me. Do not expect any more of me, even in the spirit. Otherwise I feel it, and it remains in a part of my heart which should be without preoccupations.'

The Hotel Biron had interesting inmates, including Isadora Duncan and Jean Cocteau; Rilke encouraged Rodin to set up a studio there. The large garden was visible from Rilke's studio window, in front of which he placed a baroque table given him by Rodin. On it lay neat piles of answered and unanswered letters, and the inevitable vase of roses; to one side stood a lectern and the Rilke coat-of-arms hung on the wall. The poet kept aloof from his neighbours, and as Cocteau emerged from parties, he would notice the 'dutiful' lights burning in Rilke's room. It was here that he wrote the requiems, *Malte Laurids Brigge* and the second volume of *New Poems:* from May 1908 to January 1910 there was an almost unbroken flow of writing.

The world of the *New Poems* has been compared, not without justification, to a museum, but it is in itself symbolic. Entering, we see the statues of Apollo, Artemis, Leda and the swan, Venus. Thanatos leads Alcestis to her fate and she, happy in her sacrifice, casts a last look on Admetus. Here are Orpheus, Hermes and Eurydice, and a study of the Buddha at Meudon. There are the figures from the Old and New Testaments: Elias in the desert, Absalom, St Sebastian, Joshua, Elijah, the prodigal son, a pietà, Christ on the Mount of Olives and on the Cross. And there are the animals: flamingoes, gazelles, a black cat, a snake and a panther. Human beings, such as a Spanish dancer and a courtesan, are less successfully portrayed.

It has been said that the kingdom of Rilke's poetry is the great democracy of things: *New Poems* bears this out, but it was not a volume readily understood by those familiar with his earlier work. God had apparently vanished. Clara had pressed on him *The Sayings of Buddha*, which Rilke had flatly refused to read, since unlike her he was not 'directly approaching the divine' but was coming away, charged with a mission to earth. The public missed the music they were used to in his poetry, and were puzzled by his choice of subject: washing a corpse, for instance, or whole verses on staircases, an entire sonnet devoted to the blue of hydrangeas. What was more, the volume was full of difficult, often invented words: 'Jäsen' (babel), 'löhren' (lour), and 'Selcher' (butcher) for example.

The second volume of *New Poems* was published in November 1908, dedicated 'A mon grand ami Auguste Rodin'. The typical Rilkean sonnet form now appears — abba / abab, cddc / cdcd, eef, gfg — as in the opening sonnet, one of his finest poems: 'Archaic Torso of Apollo'.

> We never knew the incredible head
> in which his pupils ripened, yet the torso
> glows still, like a candelabrum, where gleams
> the gaze, recoiling only to remain.
>
> Otherwise the bow of the breast could not
> blind you, nor the revolution of the hips
> pass on with a slow smile to the centre
> that carried the burden of creation.
>
> Otherwise the stone were only distortion
> beneath the transparent fall of the shoulders
> and would not shine like the hide of a beast;
>
> nor break out on every side, as does
> a star, since here there is not a single spot
> that does not see you. You must change your life.
>
> Wir kannten nicht sein unerhörtes Haupt,
> darin die Augenäpfel reiften. Aber
> sein Torso glüht noch wie ein Kandelaber,
> in dem sein Schauen, nur zurückgeschraubt,

sich hält und glänzt. Sonst könnte nicht der Bug
der Brust dich blenden, und im leisen Drehen
der Lenden könnte nicht ein Lächeln gehen
zu jener Mitte, die die Zeugung trug.

Sonst stünde dieser Stein entstellt und kurz
unter der Schultern durchsichtigem Sturz
und flimmerte nicht so wie Raubtierfelle;

und bräche nicht aus allen seinen Rändern
aus wie ein Stern: denn da ist keine Stelle,
die dich nicht sieht. Du musst dein Leben ändern.

The light intrinsic to the stone, that gives the torso its magical life, is
something that Rodin exploited in his work, and Rilke surely learnt
about its qualities from him.

Paula and her death still haunted Rilke; it was not until now, a year
after her death, that he was able to go some way towards coming to
terms with it, in the form of 'Requiem for a Friend' ('Requiem für eine
Freundin'). 'I have my dead. I let them go / and was amazed to see
them so consoled,' he began:

> Only you return:
> you touch me in passing, you walk about, you want
> to knock against something as a sign
> that you are there. O do not take from me
> what I am learning. I am right...

> Nur du, du kehrst
> zurück; du streifst mich, du gehst um, du willst
> an etwas stossen, dass es klingt von dir
> und dich verrät. O nimm mir nicht, was ich
> langsam erlern. Ich habe recht...

He addresses her almost reprovingly: the haunting is her fault, a
mistaken notion of what the dead need to do; it is up to the living to set
things in order after the shock of departure. That she should be afraid,
'and even now / are still afraid, where fear no longer counts, / and lose
a piece of your eternity by coming here, where nothing / exists as yet'
('und auch noch jetzt / den Schrecken hast, wo Schrecken nicht mehr

gilt; / dass du von deiner Ewigkeit ein Stück / verlierst und hier
hereintrittst, Freundin, hier, / wo alles noch nicht *ist'):* this 'awakens
me at night like a thief breaking in' ('dies weckt mich nachts oft wie
ein Dieb, der einbricht'). If she had been wandering as fearlessly as a
child, or was coming to him with a definite reproach, it might have
been bearable, but he sensed that she was pleading for something, and
that mute plea went right to his bones.

> Tell me, shall I travel?
> Is there something you have left behind and need?
> Shall I visit a country which you never saw . . .

> Sag, soll ich reisen? Hast du irgendwo
> ein Ding zurückgelassen, das sich quält
> und das dir nachwill? Soll ich in ein Land,
> das du nicht sahst . . .

Rilke goes on to list the things he might do in order to capture the spirit
of this unknown country, including watching animals so as to become
a part of their existence — as he had really done in Paris — and buying
fruits. This brings him to her as a painter, because in her work she had
not only understood the still-lifes she composed, but had also seen
women and children as fruits, herself as one, especially in the late self-
portraits when she was pregnant:

> And you saw yourself, at last, a fruit.
> Took off your clothes, and went
> before the mirror, and let yourself
> down into it, all but your glance.
> That remained great and did not say:
> that is me; no, but: this is.
> So incurious was your gaze at last,
> and so unpossessive, so truly poor,
> that it no longer wanted even you: holy.

> Und sahst dich selbst zuletzt wie eine Frucht,
> nahmst dich heraus aus deinen Kleidern, trugst
> dich vor den Spiegel, liessest dich hinein
> bis auf dein Schäuen; das blieb gross davor
> und sagte nicht: das bin ich; nein: dies ist.

So ohne Neugier war zuletzt dein Schaun
und so besitzlos, von so wahrer Armut,
dass es dich selbst nicht mehr begehrte: heilig.

From that pure gaze he returned to the world of sap and will, as she had done, a return that had killed her. Then it seems to him that she is in the room, he is unafraid and asks her to step into the candlelight, to stay a while with him in silence:

Look at this rose on my desk.
Is not the light about it just as
timid as the light round you?
It should not be here either.

Komm her; wir wollen eine Weile still sein.
Sieh diese Rose an auf meinem Schreibtisch;
ist nicht das Licht um sie genau so zaghaft
wie über dir: sie dürfte auch nicht hier sein.

He fights for comprehension, asking her to lament with him the manner of her dying: the tug between the artist at her painful labour of composition, day after day, to the limit of her strength, and the expectant, then delivered, mother, whose image in the mirror after child-birth showed 'the lovely wiles of Everywoman, happily / donning her jewels and settling her hair' ('die schöne Täuschung jeder Frau, die gern / Schmuck umnimmt und das Haar kämmt und verändert'). Rilke honestly felt that she had failed to 'die her own death', that she had been disloyal to her own deepest feelings, which may have been the cause of her returning. But in the penultimate section of the poem, Rilke comes out with a reason for this haunting: Paula feels that proper observance of her death has been lacking, she needs real mourning. He implies that this has been missing because no one loved her in the right way, least of all her husband — who withdrew her from herself — in whom Rilke accuses every man. The suffering of such 'love' has lasted too long, he said; it is too difficult for us (to whom was he referring?), 'this confused suffering of false love, / which, building on the years like custom, / calls itself a right . . . / Where is the man who has a right to possess?' ('das wirre Leiden von der falschen Liebe / die, bauend auf Verjährung wie Gewohnheit, / ein Recht sich nennt . . . / Wo ist ein Mann, der Recht hat auf Besitz?'). As he wrote, his ideas on love crystallized around the theme that its essential tragedy was that the lover was never to be at one with the beloved. For Rilke, the higher form of love which men must learn consisted in setting free the beloved: had he not done so with Clara? The position was genuinely held, but its advantages are clear: in pursuit of this kind of love, the evasions of emotional responsibility, the obliqueness of his powerful feelings for Paula — and other women — were explained, and his withdrawals justified. So too Otto Modersohn was judged, for forcing Paula to be a conventional wife and mother when all she wanted was a life's work, 'in spite of all, not done', says Rilke angrily. The word he had been avoiding could be released in such a context:

> For that is guilt, if anything is guilt,
> not to increase the freedom of the thing we love
> by all the freedom we can find within us.
> We have when we love only this:
> to leave each other; for to hold on
> is easy and need not first be learnt.

> Denn *das* ist Schuld, wenn irgendeines Schuld ist:
> die Freiheit eines Lieben nicht vermehren
> um alle Freiheit, die man in sich aufbringt.
> Wir haben, wo wir lieben, ja nur dies:
> einander lassen; denn dass wir uns halten,
> das fällt uns leicht, und ist nicht erst zu lernen.

What he had been articulating for himself in the 'Requiem', Rilke concluded, Paula probably already knew: 'Women suffer: loving means loneliness' because 'somewhere there is an ancient enmity / between human life and any great work' ('Die Frauen leiden: lieben heisst allein sein . . . Denn irgendwo ist eine alte Feindschaft / zwischen dem Leben und der grossen Arbeit'). He had said earlier in the poem that the way he wanted to keep her was the way she had placed herself within the mirror, deeply in touch with herself 'and far from all else'. The prevalence of the word 'mirror' in Rilke's poetry, though it was no doubt related to his own narcissist tendency, implied more than that: it came to stand for the other dimension in which life and death were a unity; for reality, and at the same time, for pure seeing. An artist — poet or painter — had to cultivate the same power to reflect all he saw and give everything back. Now Rilke restored Paula to her mirror:

> Go! Be dead with the dead
> if you can. The dead have work to do.
> And, if it is not disturbing, help me
> as sometimes remote things do, in me.

> Komm nicht zurück. Wenn du's erträgst, so sei
> tot bei den Toten. Tote sind beschäftigt.
> Doch hilf mir so, dass es dich nicht zerstreut,
> wie mir das Fernste manchmal hilft: in mir.

Rilke had regarded himself for some time as the spokesman for women in matters of love; he responded intuitively to the extensive literature of one-sided passion, notably in the case of Alforcorado, but also for instance in his translations of sonnets by the sixteenth-century Lyonnaise poet, Louise Labé. It is difficult to judge how much of this amounted to making a virtue of necessity. Such charming partisanship no doubt furthered his career by attracting a great deal of female patronage, and if one made it a duty to leave the beloved, then one need never be bound to the detriment of one's work. Yet Rilke's constant strictures on the dilettante habits of male lovers, ruined as human beings 'by the easy exercise of mastery', may imply that he feared himself to be all too capable of such casual relationships. So he set up the ultimate obstacle to the kind of mutually sustaining love one might consider worthwhile — involving sexuality and parenthood and some form of domestic life — by declaring that even the best lovers must part, and that what looks like loss is gain. Such a view did not preclude, indeed even encouraged, romance. And it gave a special poignancy to his loss of Paula.

This theory of parting was both wilful and a real attempt to school himself to the solitude that had proved the most fruitful condition for creation. Rilke dilated on the subject in a letter to Elisabeth Freiin Schenk zu Schweinsberg, 4 November 1909:

> Why do people who love one another leave one another before it is necessary? Perhaps because the necessity may appear and challenge at any moment. Being together and loving one

another is something so provisional. Behind it in each, often
denied, often admitted, lurks the peculiar certainty that
everything out of the ordinary must be experienced alone, by
the individual (almost singly), and be borne and overcome by
him. The moment when we die, which brings home to us all a
realization of this truth, is only one of these times, and not at
all exceptional. We are constantly changing, in a manner which
is perhaps no less intense than the newness that death brings,
and just as we must leave each other at these particular
moments of change, so we should, strictly speaking, give each
other up each moment and not restrain one another.... This
fearful truth is at the same time our most fruitful and most
sacred.... Perhaps, even, one can only develop and to some
extent complete this thing we have in common, and which we
call love, when alone and separate.... People who love each
other in this way surround themselves with infinite dangers, but
they are safe from the minor risks which have frayed and
wrecked the beginnings of so many great affections.

'People who love each other' do not always 'leave each other', but to
say 'often' or 'sometimes' or 'are forced to' would have weakened
Rilke's case, which was that in the spirit there must be a loosening, or
at least no possessiveness. Such explanations may have been efforts to
absolve himself of responsibility for his own failures with women he
had loved, with Clara, Paula, even Lou. Had he not increased the
freedom of the thing he loved by all the power he could find within
him, and thus gained absolution through the 'Requiem'? Afraid of the
new realm Paula opened up for him, and afraid of his own guilt, he had
given her freedom to leave the earth. At the end, Rilke had become
aware that it was not Paula who was haunting him, but he himself who
was calling up her shade, being possessive beyond the grave. For the
moment his conscience was at rest: the only woman he had not called a
star became just that.

The same month, Rilke wrote a requiem for Wolf Graf von
Kalckreuth, who had shot himself in October 1906, aged nineteen.
Rilke had not known him personally, but Kalckreuth was a friend of
the artists at Worpswede, himself a poet and translator of Baudelaire
and Verlaine. The poem to his memory was in a sense complementary
to the one for Paula: with knowledge of art's transforming power, the
young man might have learned not to despair, learned how to

persevere, as Paula had; though Rilke had seen both the immature and the maturing destroyed. 'Who talks of victory?' he asks at the end of the second requiem: 'To endure is all'.

VIII

The Unspeakable Fears

Crisis was at hand in Rilke's own life, a crisis of belief. Death had made it more urgent than ever that he should grapple with his fears, to relive the childhood which he had always thought must be relived in order to root out its poison, leaving nothing unsaid but reducing everything to its proper proportions.

The technique which he had evolved for his poems was not suitable for a novel: the minute and exhaustive note-taking would have had to be on an incredible scale. Rilke imagined a dialogue between a young girl and a young man. The latter began to talk about a friend of his, a Dane called Malte Laurids Brigge, who often came to see him although they did not know each other very well. When Malte died, he left behind notebooks and a diary. The girl said she would like to read it, and he showed her snatches. The figure of Malte, suggested to Rilke by the death from brain-fever of a Norwegian poet, Sigbjorn Obstfelder (1866-1900), now developed. He first made his appearance in a manuscript Rilke was working at in Rome, in February 1904. It became obvious that the notebooks were the really interesting part of the tale, and the introductory characters were dropped.

At the beginning, action alternates between Malte's life in Paris and his childhood in Denmark, where the decisive event was the death of his paternal grandfather. The description of that witnesses to the deep effect of his Uncle Jaroslav's death on Rilke; he remembered going into the death-room only to find a stranger in it, walking up and down in riding boots. The noise of the boots was terrible in a room where death ruled. Rilke could remember too the death of his own father, and perhaps it was this that inspired the scene in which the old man's heart is pierced in order to confirm that he is dead. Malte feels that it is his heart, 'our heart', which is thus pierced, leaving a scarlet, mouth-like wound in his father's chest, from which the blood twice oozes.

Grouped around Malte are the shadowy figures of other dead people: Christine Brahe, who walks through the room as the family sits at dinner, and is acknowledged by them; his mother's sister Ingeborg; and most incredibly, the materialization of the spirit of a neighbouring house which had burnt down. There was no limit set to Malte's apprehension.

The novel includes all that the protagonist remembers, all that he reads and thinks. Historical personages are as real as his own recent ancestors, and they in turn as real or unreal as people encountered in the streets. Rilke's intention may have been comparable with Proust's, but he was able to impose not the slightest hint of a pattern on *Malte*. Perhaps it belongs most clearly to the genre of the fantastic.

If Malte had been reduced to absolute poverty, perhaps he would have struggled against his own demons and dispelled them, he might have subjected himself to the discipline of work in order to live. Although family resources had disintegrated, Ulsgaard and Urnekloster in which he had spent his childhood had gone to strangers, a pittance remained which permitted Malte to live in the Latin Quarter in Paris, like some beach-comber. He feels himself to be the last representative of his race, and senses his blood becoming thin. His consciousness, through his dead ancestors, flares up in an agony of susceptibility. Malte's mother had died when he was young, but had been responsible for his belief in the incursion of the supernatural into everyday existence.

Paris for Malte is the spectral city of Strindberg, the city 'douloureuse et quasi morte' of Rimbaud. He cannot give up his country habit of sleeping with the window open:

> Electric street-cars run through my room. Cars drive over me. A door slams; somewhere a window falls. I hear the great panes laughing and the little cracks sniggering. Then, suddenly, a dull muffled sound from the other side of the house. Someone is coming up the stairs. Coming up without stopping. Is there. There for a long time. Passes. And the street again. A girl screams: oh quiet, I've had enough!

It is also the Paris of May, with girls in white and streaming veils for confirmation, but most of all it is the dark Paris, the Paris wherein Rilke followed two lovers one day, thinking he had found something beautiful, only to become aware that they were walking into a morgue. They approached a dead body on a slab, that of a young girl with dripping hair, like the live young girl. What name were they seeking? What would they do now? They suddenly looked at each other and kissed. There is a lengthy description of the onset of an epileptic fit in a passer-by, whom Malte follows until he falls, writhing with an invisible opponent who holds him in a wrestling lock. 'And what did the old woman want of him who had crawled out of some hole, with a night drawer in which a few buttons and needles rolled? Why did she walk by and watch him?' What could be done about any of them?

As Malte lies in bed, feverish, all the fears that had assailed him in childhood return: the fear that some number in his head should go on multiplying until there was no more space in his whole body to hold it. The fear that the bed in which he was lying should be granite, black granite. The fear that he might shout out, which would bring people running to break down his door. The fear of betraying himself by confessing all that made him afraid. And the fear of not being able to say a word, because everything is unutterable.

Like Goethe's Werther, Malte became the other self of his creator. Just as Goethe had used real letters, so Rilke mined his own correspondence for his novel. The fever fears are undoubtedly a re-creation of his childhood experience, but in writing to Countess Manon zu Solms-Laubach Rilke refused to identify himself completely with Malte, who had developed 'into a figure which, quite detached from me, acquired existence and personality, and interested me the more intensely, the more differentiated it became from myself' (11 April 1907). Nevertheless, passages remembered by Malte from Jacobsen, Hermann Bang, Hofmannsthal and Gide, were also those Rilke admired.

Lou Andreas-Salomé gives an interesting picture of Rilke at this time. She said she was amazed that there were no signs of age on his face. It actually appeared not to be his. The eyes were wide and afraid, as if wondering what had happened; the nose, mouth and chin were strangers to them. She asked, as she had done in their early encounters, whether he was 'Rainer' or 'der Andere', though the impression of his being two people was rarer than it had been. And he replied: 'Ich bin jetzt der Andere' ('I am the other one'; like Rimbaud, 'Je est un autre'). Rilke wrote to Lou on 28 December 1911:

No one but you can distinguish, and determine precisely whether Malte — who was in fact created from the same dangers as threatened me — perished to save me from perishing, or whether the *Notebooks* did not thrust me out into

the current, which is carrying me off... Malte in a certain
sense exhausted all my resources, wasted the patrimony of
substance and the energy of my life. There is nothing in me
which was not already in him and in his heart.

In the second part of the book there is an endless procession of
historical figures: Christian IV of Denmark and the false Tsar Grishka
Otrepyev; Pope John XXII and Charles IV of France; Charles the Bold
and the Count de Ligny; John of Gaunt and the French poet Felix
Arvers. Notable female lovers follow, the roll-call of the intelligent
and long-suffering: Sappho, Heloise, Louise Labé, Gaspara Stampa,
Julie de Lespinasse, Eleonora Duse... and Abelone, the young aunt
with whom Malte falls in love. A girl like her appears at the end, to
sing a song in a drawing-room in Venice. In the song there are the
familiar motifs of the inevitable betrayal of feeling once the beloved
has surrendered, the fear of being possessed and of possessing, the
elevation of separation: 'because I never held you close, I hold you
forever'.

There is nothing quite like *Malte Laurids Brigge* in modern literature.
Parallels have been drawn between Rilke and Gide, much of whose
philosophy — especially in *L'Enfant prodigue,* which he translated, and
Les nourritures terrestres — Rilke made his own. Yet closer parallels are to
be found in some of the essays of W.B. Yeats, particularly that on
magic in the volume *Ideas of Good and Evil.* Both poets ignored arbitrary
divisions in the human mind, seeing it functioning according to the
laws of image and symbol, not of logic and concept; they apprehended
not a merely occult world, but a timeless world of the spirit.
Unfortunately Rilke was unable to stand outside his own fears, to rid
himself of them like the man in Yeats's essay by 'cutting off their
heads'.

Malte was certainly a blood-letting, but it was not the final answer,
did not transform Rilke's world. That process did not take place for
many years. He never succeeded in dealing with people, or in seeing
into people, as he had managed with things and with animals. If *Malte*
was the attempt, as he indicated to Rodin, it was also the failure to
make of his characters more than apparitions. It has been said that the
novel could have been written by one of Dostoievsky's characters,
who also live in an atmosphere of hallucination, but not by
Dostoievsky himself. In a letter to Countess Lili Kanitz-Menar, Rilke
said that on completing *Malte* he felt 'rather as Raskolnikov did after

his deed', having accomplished it *'with what strength?* I ask myself; *with what right?* I would almost like to ask...' (7 September 1910).

Rilke's genius was lyrical, and he dissolved Malte's being in a wave of lyricism that constituted his impressions of the world. The excessive formlessness and vagueness Rilke had avoided in his poetry, thanks to Rodin's example, he fell prey to in this novel. Edmond Jaloux, in his study of Rilke (1927), sees it sympathetically as the 'search for the intimate rhythm which touches upon everything just at the moment in which it is being transformed', and suggests that the strength of the novelist 'consists in taking the measure of the soul during those moments when it escapes from its normal forms and advances into the unknown'.

The novel ends with a version of the tale of the Prodigal Son, whose escape and return is bound up with an exploration of the meaning of love. Did he himself not know how to love? Or had he forgotten? Or did he realize only too late that he had loved? But Rilke is less concerned with the Son's ability to give than his refusal to accept what he saw as the wrong kind of love. *The Notebooks* finishes: 'What did they know about him? He was extremely difficult to love, and he felt that one alone was capable of it, but He was not yet willing.' Like the Prodigal Son who, he wrote, had fled from love in order to learn to love selflessly, and forsaking human love had turned to God, Rilke was convinced that the distance between himself and God was too great. The Son, he recounts, almost forgot God in the labour of approaching Him, part of which was that living through childhood again which Rilke himself was doing in *Malte.* It becomes increasingly difficult to separate the three figures: the Prodigal, Malte, the author. Their journeys are more and more in the nature of flights, and they long for a home. The Prodigal returns only to find his family making gestures of forgiveness, failing to understand anything of his mission. Rilke, like Malte, had still to travel over Europe with 'a trunk and a box of books'. Years later, in the eighth *Elegy,* Rilke described the fortunate 'free animal', always walking towards God, unshackled by the self-consciousness of humans; Malte being a prime example of one thus bound.

> And yet in the wakeful, warm creature
> there is weight of care and melancholy.
> For he too is troubled by what often
> overwhelms us — memory,

as if what we strive for, had once
been nearer, truer, and its accession
infinitely gentle. Here all is detachment
and there it was breath. After the first home
the second, to him, is hybrid and vain.

Und doch ist in dem wachsam warmen Tier
Gewicht und Sorge einer grossen Schwermut.
Denn ihm auch haftet immer an, was uns
oft überwältigt, — die Erinnerung,
als sei schon einmal das, wonach man drängt,
näher gewesen, treuer und sein Anschluss
unendlich zärtlich. Hier ist alles Abstand,
und dort wars Atem. Nach der ersten Heimat
ist ihm die zweite zwitterig und windig.

IX

Duino

On a visit to Paris in December 1909, Princess Marie von Thurn und Taxis called on her friend the Comtesse de Noailles, and was surprised to learn that the latter had been receiving unusual letters from a certain Rainer Maria Rilke. Princess Marie informed the Comtesse that Rilke was one of the best young poets in German, and that although she did not know him personally, she thought a meeting could be arranged. Thus Rilke met the Princess for the first time when he accepted her invitation to tea on the 13th of December. She noted that his manners were excellent, that his shyness was combined with an air of distinction, that he appeared rather 'ugly but very nice'. Shortly after Rilke's arrival the Comtesse was announced; dressed like an Egyptian goddess, she walked in and transfixed him with questions: 'Ah, Monsieur Rilke, what do you think of love? What do you think of death?'

The three discussed the merits of contemporary poets, and the Comtesse asked whether Rilke did not find technique a great deal of trouble when writing his poetry, to which he replied that the inspiration simply came. This was the line he consistently took concerning composition, but it takes no account of his preparation, nor of revision. When he left, the two ladies laughed over the apparently intimidating effect of the Comtesse; at the same time, Princess Marie was impressed and touched by Rilke. She became the last and most munificent of his patronesses.

Malte Laurids Brigge, essentially completed on 20 October 1909, was still in manuscript and scattered through various notebooks. Rilke wrote to his publisher saying that he was looking for a typist to whom he could dictate the work, whereupon Kippenberg invited him to stay in Leipzig and make use of his own secretary. In her memoir, Frau Kippenberg described her impression of the poet at their first encounter in January 1910. His dark eyes were of 'a clear blue such as certain children have', but his nose was the dominant facial feature, long and powerful; the whole was reminiscent of a well-bred hunting dog. His mouth was surrounded by a Chinese-style spiral moustache, and Frau Kippenberg noted that Rilke's colour and expression changed very rapidly during the course of conversation, so that he seemed to have several faces. She found him punctilious in the matter of arrivals and departures. In the course of his three weeks with them, Frau Kippenberg observed that he did not seem to be striving for mystical experience, nor for any form of depersonalization; on the contrary, Rilke was rich in sensory perceptions, and seemed anxious to be in touch with the divine only in order to return to the world and his work.

The circumstances of 1910, with Rilke shuttling about Europe, were scarcely conducive to work. His address-book at this time contained about twelve hundred names. It had become his practice on arriving in a strange town to find out who were the old families and to read up their histories, partly out of genuine interest in the past, partly because he found it flattered his hosts. Princess Marie invited him to her home on the Adriatic, and in April Rilke arrived at Duino for the first time. He said he had always known that there must be a castle somewhere in the vicinity; the environment was full of literary associations, with Vergil, with Petrarch, whose grave Rilke visited in nearby Arqua, with Dante who had once visited Pagana delle Torre, Patriarch of Aquilea; at the foot of the cliffs on which Schloss Duino stood, jutted out a rock known locally as 'Dante's Rock'. On this visit Rilke met Rudolf Kassner (1873-1959), the cultural philosopher who was also a guest of the Princess, but he did not stay long before moving on to Venice, back to Paris, and in August he joined the Princess in her other home in Austria, Schloss Lautschin; at the end of the month he was with the Baroness Nádherný at Schloss Janowitz. From Bohemia on 30 August he wrote revealingly to Princess Marie:

> ... Perhaps I shall now learn to become a little human; hitherto my art has really only come into being at the price of my always insisting on *things;* ... I am a little horrified when I think of all the violence I put forth in *Malte,* how in my consequent desperation I plunged clean through to the back of things ... I do not think that anyone has more clearly experienced how much art goes against nature; it is the most passionate inversion of the natural order, the way back from the Infinite, the road on which all honest earthly things are moving in a direction

opposite to oneself; one now sees them in their complete shape, their faces approach, their movement acquires particularity: yes, but who is one then that has the right to move in this direction against them all, this eternal reverse, with which one deceives them by allowing them to suppose that one has already arrived somewhere, reached some end, and now had the leisure to return?...

In November Rilke left for Algiers and Tunis, whence he wrote to Clara and Ruth, giving a description of the promising glitter of the souks:

... and when in the evening a single lantern burns and waves to and fro, as though excited at the presence of all it lights up, then a Thousand and One Nights become all one had expected, wished and hoped, and Christmas is no longer so difficult to imagine. In the Souk of Perfumers we have a friend already. If you shake hands with him it lasts the whole day... I buy Geranium Essence from him...

But the glamour did not last; Rilke was unwell, tense and in financial difficulty. Nevertheless he went on to the valley of the Nile, and February found him at Shepheard's Hotel in Cairo. Reviewing the year in a letter to Lou on 28 December 1911, Rilke wrote of the expedition:

Unfortunately there was so little in me that was fitted for it that I lost seat and hold and finally only tagged along like someone thrown by a bolting horse, bumping over the ground by one stirrup.... a little of the East was instilled into me, on the Nile boat I even came to terms with Arabic, and the Museum in Cairo did perhaps, after all, make something of me, confused as I was when I entered.

He finally took shelter with Baron Jacob and Baroness May Knoop in Heluan, where Clara had been housed in 1907. Egypt made a profound impression on Rilke, although it was some time before that emerged in his work. In a letter to Clara he asked, 'What moment of windless calm existed in the great period of Egypt? What God held his breath to allow these men at the time of Amenhotep to exist? Where did they suddenly come from and how did time close again behind them?...' (10 February 1911). By 1913 he had sufficiently recovered his enthusiasm to consider joining Professor Steindorff's expedition to the

Nubian desert, along with the Kippenbergs and Lou Andreas-Salomé. But on 6 March 1911 he was writing to Kippenberg from Paris: 'I wish for nothing, nothing, but that I may be able at last to return to quiet achievement, to that modest, regular life that was possible in this same house before the days of the rue de Varenne.'

The summer in Paris had its curious episode: Rilke's encounter with Marthe Hennebert, both in their way 'strays'. He met Marthe when walking in a poor quarter of the city; she was seventeen, beautiful, hungry, alone in the world and in such despair that she thought of taking her life. Rilke took her under his wing, giving her books to read and reading her his own poems in translation, astonished by her intuitive understanding. As he later wrote to a friend: 'I don't know whether any human being has ever similarly shown me to what extent a temperament can spontaneously unfold itself if it is given a bit of living space, a bit of quiet, a tiny bit of favourable climate' (26 September 1919). Rilke could not assume entire responsibility for her, and wanted to put her into the care of a friend, Frau Werndl; Marthe at first refused, saying that she preferred to remain with him even if she had to curl up on the doormat like a dog. His wishes must have prevailed, however, since he wrote to von Gebsattel on 14 January 1912:

> Marthe (of her I only hear indirectly from Frau W. who, it seems, has a more lively concern for her than ever), Marthe is learning to cook and has talent for it, in the evening she draws and for that, too, she has an eye that is scarcely credible; now and then she visits the theatre with Frau W., all this, in her, becomes pure life, finds innumerable receptive places in her nature, — it will be a marvel.

Rilke was still fretting over finance. His travels were expensive, especially as he would now stay only at the best hotels, given his obsession with cleanliness, his desire for quiet and good service. Certainly his royalties were substantial by this time: *Early Poems,* issued in 1909, was reprinted for a third time in 1913; *Malte* sold out in its first year, running to a third edition in 1918; the *Requiems* sold well. By August 1914, *The Book of Hours* was in its seventh edition, *New Poems I* in its third (having sold six thousand copies), *New Poems II* in its second, *Tales of God* in its fourth; the monograph on Rodin had sold ten thousand copies and the *Comet* had sold forty thousand. Rilke's patrons von der Heydt and Count Kessler, joined by Rudolf Kassner and the unfailing Kippenberg, agreed to make him an allowance for 1912-14 in addition to any royalties. The poet wrote to thank his publisher on 27 September 1911:

> Your alacrity has again accomplished the impossible. I shall probably, if all goes well, be taken care of for the next quarter, but my wife is taking Ruth away from her grandmother, a change which, I think, promises to be for the best. She is to go to school in Munich. I would like to be helpful about this, and can be so this quarter, the more I am invited about...

In October he was given notice to leave his flat in the rue de Varenne, but was not homeless thanks to Princess Marie, who sent her car to collect him in Paris and convey him to Duino, where they could both spend the winter. Rilke remained there until May 1912, in fact alone much of the time for a critical period in his work.

At first he found the retreat a relief. 'What is a god without a cloud?' he wrote; 'Duino is the cloud of my being'. His room was in a quiet corner of the castle, with windows on three sides overlooking the sea and a hidden stairway leading to the oratorium. Not far away was the Princess's sitting-room, the walls covered with water-colours, etchings, drawings including a Tiepolo of centaurs, the head of a nymph in the Veronese style, with an Umbrian Madonna beside it, and Genoese hangings; it was filled with flowers, Duinese roses and cyclamen from the Carso. Rilke would appear here at night with candles, to begin work on a translation of the *Vita Nuova* with the Princess. Kassner was again a guest at the castle, a man for whom Rilke had infinite admiration. The two met fairly frequently, in Paris or at Duino, and Rilke observed to Kippenberg: 'He is really the only one with whom I can do anything. He is the only one to whom it occurs to use a little of what is feminine in me' (1 May 1910). The company made excursions together, and the Princess and Rilke drove to Friuli at his suggestion, to see the house in which he had spent a childhood summer. It was empty, the garden was overgrown; they went round to the back of the house to find the large stone beside which he used to play with Amelia — and on it lay a bouquet of violets. 'Take it,' said the Princess, 'it must be meant for you.' They went to see the Tiepolo frescoes in the Palazzo at Udine and to Castelfranco. And Rilke, who had never set much store by music as an art, was gradually being converted by listening to Beethoven, played on the great terrace at Duino by the

Quartetto Triestino. As idyllic as it sounds, especially in Princess Marie's memoir, Rilke was not happy. He took it into his head to move to an old pavilion in the garden, which was without water or heating or furniture; Miss Greenham, the housekeeper, was horrified at the idea, and Rilke was persuaded to keep to the castle.

Life there became something of an ordeal for him, and under its strain he began writing long letters to Lou after a break of nearly two years, the first on 28 December. It distressed him that he should be longing for human companionship since the completion of *Malte,* when he had been independent of that need in his best period, writing the *New Poems* in Paris. 'Are the symptoms those of the long convalescence which is my life? Are they the signs of a new illness?' He felt like a kind of hermit crab, alone in the little fort with its flagstone courtyard, sealed off by a high wall. Two days later he wrote to Princess Marie:

> Loneliness is a true elixir, it forces the disease completely to the
> surface: first one has to get bad, worse, worst... then, though,
> one gets well. I creep about for the whole day in the thickets
> of my life and scream like a savage and clap my hands: — you
> wouldn't believe what hair-raising creatures then fly up.

In the New Year Rilke was considering psychoanalysis, discussing it with Lou and with Emil von Gebsattel. The latter became an intimate of Lou's, having fallen in love with her at the Weimar psychoanalytic congress of 1911, at which time he counted Clara Rilke among his patients. Clara urged her husband to undergo treatment; Rilke expressed his strong reservations in a letter to von Gebsattel on 14 January:

> I always have the idea that my work is really nothing but a
> self-treatment of this kind, how else could I (even at the age of
> ten or twelve) have got down to working at all? My wife,
> from whom I receive only short and infrequent letters,
> thinks... that a sort of cowardice is frightening me away from
> psychoanalysis; for, as she puts it, it would be commensurate
> with the 'trusting', the 'pious' side of my nature to take it upon
> myself, — but that is not right; it is precisely my, if one may
> say so, piousness which holds me back from this intervention,
> from this great clearing-up which Life does *not* do, — from this
> correcting of all the pages Life has hitherto written...

... I am nevertheless moved by nothing so much as by the incomprehensible, the stupendous marvel of my own being which was so impossibly biassed from the start and which yet travelled from salvation to salvation ... whenever I think of not writing anymore this fact alone dismays me, the fact of not having recorded the absolutely miraculous line of this so strangely lived life.... Can you understand, my friend, that I am afraid of disturbing by any sort of arrangement and supervision, however palliative, a much higher order which I would be bound to justify by all that has happened, even if it condemns me to perdition?

When he wrote to Lou on 20 January, he suggested that 'something perilously close to a disinfected soul' would be the result of psychoanalysis, and said that he found himself 'thoroughly insupportable on purely physical grounds'; he felt so unwell, 'my body is running the risk of becoming the caricature of my spirituality'. By telegram and letter she confirmed his instinct not to undergo analysis.

In the midst of this agitated correspondence, Rilke sent a note to Princess Marie accompanying a green notebook she had given him, 'obdurately inscribed with the first work in Duino (and the first for ages!), for which precisely it was made' (21 January 1912). Walking on the battlements one windy morning, he seemed to hear out of the teeth of the Bora the words: 'Wer, wenn ich schriee, hörte mich denn aus der Engel Ordnungen?' — 'Who if I screamed would hear me then, out of the ranks of the angels?' Nothing else came, but back in his room, Rilke found he could continue with what was to be the first of the *Duino Elegies:* 'And even if one of them took me to his heart: I should die from his stronger presence' ('und gesetzt selbst, es nähme / einer mich plötzlich ans Herz: ich verginge von seinem / stärkeren Dasein').

Perhaps it was this unexpected return to writing — the second elegy was also drafted at the end of January, and the third at least begun early in 1912 — that led Rilke to write quite firmly to von Gebsattel on 24 January that he had no wish for a real change, 'no relief save that which is inherent in endurance and the ultimate triumph'. Perhaps he had exaggerated his fears, certainly he felt that 'if my devils were driven out my angels also would receive a slight ... shock, and, you see, I cannot let it come to that pass at any price'. Even writing, or the discovery of Goethe's 'Harzreise im Winter' — 'sheer magnificence' — or his pleasure in reading Froissart, could not compensate for the way Rilke felt his spirit shackled by his body. He wrote despairingly to Lou on 1 March:

> There are days when I look at the whole of creation with the fear that some agony may break out in it and cause it to scream, so great is my terror of the abuse which the body, in so many things, wreaks on the soul, which has peace in the animals and safety only in the angels.

Yet there was another experience to put in the balance, something that went so deep it was another year before Rilke attempted to articulate it, in the fragment *Erlebnis,* written in Spain at the end of 1912. One day at Duino he had been gazing at the prospect of trees in the castle garden, leaning against an olive-tree, when suddenly he seemed to feel himself in another life, stormed by 'everything that had ever suffered and loved and lived'. The very air seemed alive, and he to have reached 'the other side of Nature'. In this state,

> he was able to observe how all objects yielded themselves to him more distantly and, at the same time, somehow more truly; this might have been due to his vision, which was no longer directed forwards until, out there in the open, it thinned away; he was looking, over his shoulder, as it were, backwards at things, and their for him now concluded existence took on a bold, sweet after-taste, as though everything had been spiced with a trace of the blossom of parting.

Its essence was this simultaneous recognition of the separate identity and life of things, given value by their very transience and the constant presence of death. The fragment concludes: 'Saying to himself from time to time that it could not last, he nevertheless had no fear about the cessation of this extraordinary condition, as though, just as from music, all that was to be expected from it was an infinitely legitimate close'. And these were the intuitions to be expressed and confirmed in his poetry.

X

The Wanderer

In the spring Rilke escaped to Venice, again indebted to Princess Marie as she put at his disposal a small apartment in the seventeenth-century Ca' Valmarana. It was in Venice that he at last met Eleonora Duse, for whom years ago he had remodelled *The White Princess* and to whom he dedicated the play. For her three-week stay they were constantly in each other's company, together with her companion Signora Poletti: 'I ate with them in the house on the Zattere,' Rilke reported to Princess Marie, 'it was companionable, full of friendship, full of intimacy, and once more a pure significance came out of the simplest things and passed over into greatness' (12 July 1912). Also travelling with the Duse were the Princess's brother, a devoted friend, and the actor Moissi, who wished to be her impresario. The tensions in the Duse's entourage were considerable, and Rilke found himself caught up in them, witnessing a tragic decline such as he saw in Rodin. Signora Poletti was writing a play, *Ariadne,* intended to restore the Duse to her pinnacle of fame; Rilke realised that his own play, which would have to be translated and reworked, would not do: 'The Duse — if it is not too late — can only portray something perfect... But where is this work, and what will keep her from ruining herself beforehand?' (letter to Princess Marie, 3 August).

He could not prevent it, indeed became affected by her own despair, although he energetically pursued the matter of founding a Duse-Theatre, or at least finding a suitable play. Rilke maintained 'that glorious sympathy with suns that set', but could not help being relieved by the company's whirlwind departure.

Back at Duino in September, perhaps because he was in low spirits and was ready to cater to the Princess's fascination with psychic phenomena, Rilke began to indulge in séances. He had already declared himself haunted by the ghosts of three young women, the Princess's sisters Theresina, Raymondine and Polyxene. One evening the Princess, her son Pascha and Rilke experimented with *planchette,*

89

with Pascha holding the pencil. Rilke wrote down his questions in silence; the unknown woman who 'spoke' in reply did so in a manner very akin to his own, urging Rilke to go to Toledo. Princess Marie later thought that there was some kind of telepathy between Rilke and her son, a transference of thought as Rilke had been speaking about Spain and his desire to visit the country. Such dabbling with the occult scarcely did justice to his real conviction that the living made too clear a distinction between themselves and the dead, whereas angels often did not know one state from the other.

A year previously Rilke had expressed his longing to go to Toledo, in a letter to Princess Marie in which he described the impression made on him by the El Grecos he had seen in Munich. His wish was realised in the winter of 1912, when he began his Spanish visit by staying in Toledo. There he found by chance the church of San Juan de los Reyes, on one of his first walks, and on its walls hung rows of the chains of liberated prisoners; the spirit had told him to search out the place 'of steel chains and bloody chains'. Just as the Russian journeys had introduced his first period of creative activity, Rilke expected the Spanish one to provide a spur for the elegies, and he wrote to a friend that he had seen immediately 'that there are many things here which I have long needed' (17 November). To Lou he wrote of Toledo that it infinitely surpassed all longing:

> There are no words to tell you how superlatively this town
> stood before me in all its untamed scenery, absolutely
> immediate, something that could not have been endured a
> moment before, chastising and comforting at once, like Moses
> when he came down from the mountain with the Tables —
> and yet gradually reminding me of all that was necessary,
> strong, pure and dependable in my life.

(19 December). He remained there four weeks before the climate got the better of him, then went on to Cordoba. The city's effect, he wrote to Princess Marie, was to confirm his tendency towards 'almost rabid' anti-Christianity; his reading of the Koran was striking responsive chords. 'Here you are supposed to be in a Christian country, well here too it has long been overpassed . . . now an immeasurable indifference reigns over all . . . The fruit is sucked dry, — all that is left for us is, speaking crudely, to spit out the rind' (17 December). Six days spent in Seville were a waste, and he had come to Ronda for its mountain air; again the surroundings were stunning, but Rilke admitted to the

Princess that he was living like any tourist in an excellent English hotel, 'and yet I am shameless enough to give it out that I am travelling in Spain'. While he despaired in Spain over the loss of his powers, the trip was to prove of vital importance to his work, as he reiterated in later letters, and he did begin the *Sixth Elegy* there. But in early January, he transcribed for Lou an entry in his notebook, and lamented that the elegies were a 'bitterly truncated' fragment of the poetry of which he had once been capable:

> Really he was long since free, and if anything prevented him from dying, it was perhaps only the circumstance that he had somehow overlooked death on the way, so that he did not, like other people, have to go on to reach it, but to turn back.

Rilke returned to Paris, to a flat in the rue Campagne-Première, 'an incomparable return'. He had spent a week in Madrid, and had been 'mad enough to buy two lovely Greco photographs, and the book on Greco by Cossios' he wrote to Kippenberg, who had to send him twenty-five pounds for the return journey, and more to help Rilke establish himself in Paris. It was in this period that the friendship with Rodin finally came to grief. The director of the Mannheim Museum had commissioned a bust of Rodin from Clara Rilke, and in 1912 Rilke had been their intermediary, getting Rodin's qualified assent to a sitting. When he announced Clara's imminent arrival in March 1913, Rodin flatly refused to co-operate. Nevertheless he seems to have been kind to Clara, because Rilke sent him a fulsome letter of thanks for the morning Rodin had given them in May. A few days later, Rodin at the last minute withdrew his consent to photographs of his work being reproduced in a new edition of Rilke's monograph, which led to a quarrel that was never patched up. Less dramatically, Rilke and Clara were also increasingly estranged.

When Princess Marie inquired after Marthe, Rilke replied that she had slipped from the surveillance of Frau Werndl, and had gone to live with a Russian painter 'as a sister, infinitely relieved not to love him'. The man was a kind of savage, speaking a primitive Siberian dialect mixed with Italian. They were living in a completely disorganized way, not eating very often; the painter had some money but it would soon disappear because of his good nature and negligence; Rilke thought that Marthe was suffering and wasting away. Yet he felt helpless, neither wise nor passionate:

I am no lover at all, it touches me only from the outside,
perhaps because no one has ever really shaken me to the
depths, perhaps because I do not love my mother. I stand there
quite poverty-stricken before this rich little creature, in whom
a person with a nature less cautious and imperilled than mine
has been of recent years could have blossomed forth and found
boundless delight. All love is an effort for me, performance,
surmenage, only in relation to God do I have any facility, for to
love God means entering, going, rising, resting and always
being in God's love.

His relations with women, or his inability to sustain them, were much
on his mind: after writing the above letter on Good Friday, on Easter
Monday he composed one to Paula's brother on the publication of her
letters and diaries:

You know, dear Dr Becker, how much the destiny of her
passing away shook me to my inmost depths. There may have
been other circumstances which played their part in this,
nevertheless that she, who was so extremely lovable in her
heart, should have left us so early, and in so shattering a
manner: this was probably the cause that for many years death
outweighed life for me ... Forgive me, I am talking a lot about
myself, but it struck home to me.

The one steady female influence on him was Lou, at whose house in
Göttingen Rilke spent a week in mid-July, and he rejoined her in
August for the psychoanalytical congress in Munich. Lou introduced
him to Freud; Rilke passed a month in Lou's circle and reported to
Princess Marie: 'We read and discuss a lot together, and for me these
hours are even here the most significant' (15 September). For the first
time Lou met Frau Rilke, and noted in her diary that Rilke saw just
enough of himself in his hysterical mother to be dumb with horror in
her presence. In October they had two weeks of autumn walks in the
Riesengebirge near Dresden, where Rilke met Franz Werfel, an
intelligent young admirer of his work, whom Lou wished he could
think of as a son. Lou wrote from Dresden to her 'dearest mortal, dear
old Rainer': 'It was so dreadful the last day, as if I were almost chasing
you away'. He replied from Paris, on 21 October, enormously grateful
for her understanding and reassurance: 'somehow you have helped me
infinitely, the rest is now for me and the angel, if only we cling

together, he and I, and you from afar . . .'. His room in Paris reminded him of all the miseries of the summer and his inability to be content with his isolation:

> Doing a little reading, resting, looking out of the window, I could be content with everything, if only it were entirely mine again, and did not keep overflowing into longing. I am terrified when I think of how I have lived beyond myself, as though always standing at a telescope, ascribing to every passing woman a serenity that could never be found with any of them: my serenity, the serenity — once — of my loneliest hours. How often I have to recall that poem from *New Poems* called, I think, 'The Stranger' ['Der Fremde'] — how well I knew what was needed:
>
> > To leave all this behind without craving . . .
>
> [Und dies alles immer unbegehrend / hinzulassen] And I, who still do nothing but crave. — Begin over again.

XI

Hearing the Music

In the New Year of 1914, Rilke received a letter from a young woman telling him how much she had enjoyed reading his *Tales of God*. Magda von Hattingberg, later the celebrated 'Benvenuta', reproduces this opening letter in her memoir of their relationship, *Rilke and Benvenuta* (1943):

> Dear Friend:
>   Your *Tales of God* are dedicated to Ellen Key and in that wonderful dedication you say that no one could like *Tales of God* more than she, and that the book thus belongs to her. Until now I have never wished to be anyone but myself. But this once I would like to be Ellen Key to have the right to that dedication, because I really think I like the *Tales of God* better than anyone else in the world.

She went on to say that his book had given her infinite comfort and was so full of music that she wished she could express her gratitude in those terms, since 'music is my element'. There was no address on the envelope, only her name. Yet Rilke was not long in answering.

Paris, 26 January, 1914.

> Dear Friend:
>   Let me take up the rich tone, it is so natural after your letter: what a joy that you should have written it, and how good too that you found difficulty in becoming Ellen Key, which would have complicated things immeasurably. Especially as apart from the *Tales of God* we have been mutually dissatisfied with each other's work... But perhaps to you too all that I have written since seems wrong or indifferent, and I should thus send the complimentary passages in your letter to the most uncertain address of the young man who wrote about God so long ago?
>   To be frank, why should he have it?... it seems to me that

he coloured in the contours of his feelings very light-heartedly in those days; you give him much more than his due. Really, I can tell you absolutely nothing about him; perhaps after all you do him justice. In any case I have this advantage over him: however much you spoil him, he will never hear your music, it is I who will hear it, indeed, I hope so...

... Why did you not, when you were on your travels, come through Southern Spain? Ah how I would have received you, my heart would have built triumphal arch on triumphal arch for you, you would have seen your music unfolding without end, for it could only reach its destination in the depths of me, which I myself have not penetrated.

He told her about Ronda, and how he had sat staring at the sky until he felt the need to be blind in the face of such a welter of recollected images, or to have access to some new sense: music was what was needed. Benvenuta was completely enraptured by his words, which seemed to her like a song she had never heard yet had always known. It was scarcely to be believed that a stranger had written these words to her, let alone Rilke.

The correspondence developed and their discussions about music became increasingly significant. Rilke had reached a stage when the lyrical element was about to predominate over the architectonic in his work, and it was Benvenuta's mention of music that had first attracted him. He told her that he almost feared music, unless it were played in a cathedral directly to God; that it was thought that music had been forbidden in ancient Egypt, a prohibition he understood: 'It could only be performed before God, for him alone, as though only he could bear the excess and seduction of its sweetness, which would be fatal to anyone else.' Rilke was becoming conscious of a new motive power, inherent in music, to which he only had access through human mediation. Although he disliked that conception, he realized that his feelings and ideas were being answered and reciprocated by Benvenuta, a sense of companionship that gave him boundless pleasure.

He told her all about his life: his fears, his aspirations, the mixed emotions of his childhood, the way he had suddenly become aware of girls:

But one day there they were, quieter than usual: at coffee-time one could observe them, and the quietest one sat facing you.

How lovely she was!... Suddenly one wondered, Heaven
knows why, whether she had been crying recently, and then,
over all the gâteaux, your heart went out to her... It was a
very one-sided business, loving such a grown-up, thoughtful
girl;... Overwhelmed by the noble joy of the troubadours, that
first chivalric pride, first melancholy, at the thought that she
would never know...

Of his father, he said that he thought he was incapable of love, but that
to the end he had preserved a kind of heartfelt anguish over his son, in
the face of which Rilke had been almost disarmed, and which might
have cost him more than the most powerful love. He told Benvenuta
about his marriage and his child, his friendship with Rodin and their
misunderstandings, and of the demons in his own nature. Rilke saw his
own 'self' as an unconscious enemy, constantly debasing and ridiculing
his own best interests; an enemy who assumed the guise of an angel,
often in order to achieve the suppression and withdrawal from life
upon which it insisted.

Benvenuta was immensely touched to find this most sympathetic
and understanding of men suffering agonies in his own life, and did
what she could to provide some happiness. Sometimes it appeared that
she was succeeding, when his letters were light and almost joyous. He
wrote to her as he never wrote to anyone else, in a manner he
described later to Lou:

> ... a spontaneous vivacity welled up as though I had struck a
> new, brimming ebullience in my own being which now, loosed
> in an inexhaustible spate of communication... whilst I... felt
> its joyful streaming and at the same time the mysterious repose
> which seemed naturally prepared for it in the recipient. To
> keep this communication pure and limpid and to feel or think
> nothing that could be excluded by it: this suddenly... became
> the law and measure of my doing... The daily round and my
> relation to it became, in some indescribable manner, sacred and
> responsible, — and from then on a powerful confidence seized
> hold of me...   (8 June 1914)

Rilke described the neighbourhood in which he lived, the little
restaurant where he ate, the post office, bringing his environment
vividly to life for her. At other times this serene spirit was replaced by

intuitions of tragedy, as in the haunted account reminiscent of a Schnitzler story:

> Once I was away the whole day, and returned late in the evening. On the stairs in front of my door I found a great bunch of flowers brought from the country, and tall branches of peach and apple blossom, the most wonderful of all ... But I worked myself to death, for two hours, to arrange these flowers. No vase seemed tall enough for the heavy, spreading branches. Each time I thought I had finished, there were more flowers; I kept finding them on the floor, on chairs, across the books. I looked for another vase and the light was blinding me amidst the shadows, I did not find the flowers I wanted but discovered others. They looked so tired, as if they were swooning, I knelt down, put my candle on the ground and tried to untie them. When I looked up, the branches were casting a shadow on the opposite wall like a gigantic claw. And when I finally managed to finish, I knocked over the tall vase full of branches, and a flood of water poured out. Benvenuta, is there a hell? ...

Only the sheer loneliness in evidence here prevents the incident from becoming ridiculous. Letters such as these worried the young woman and she advised Rilke to see a doctor, which he steadfastly refused to do. He thought that sickness was no more anxious to linger than one was to have it stay; 'as soon as something secure is there, it wants to go itself'. Again he defended his decision not to consult Freud or another psychoanalyst by saying that his strength consisted in not imposing any control on the most secret forces within himself. Often he talked about his 'blood', interpreting the most diverse phenomena in its terms, from eyestrain — 'blood pressure on the eyes — to war, 'the flowing god of the blood'. His secret forces were perhaps more physically controlled than he realised.

Rilke began to urge a meeting, and his tone of entreaty was such that Benvenuta did suggest possible cities: Florence, Lucerne, Geneva. He chose Geneva as a place new to him and thus appropriate for their first encounter. Benvenuta, however, was suddenly called away to Berlin, the 'heavy' city of his student days where Rilke had never felt at home. As he waited the tension in his letters became almost unbearable, and in the last he suggested she might feel 'as soon as you touch me, that the gulf is unbridgeable and that the purest approach will find no echo, because some sombre and inexorable destiny is waiting...'.

He gave her the name of his hotel in Berlin, where at last they met, laughing and crying. Rilke had thought her hair was brown, but of course it had to be chestnut; he could not take his eyes off her. Unfortunately, Benvenuta was already thinking that he was scarcely human, an apparition miraculously come to earth: the very impression that he wanted to avoid and yet could not help conveying. They talked and he accompanied her part of the way home. Such was the beginning of an episode which was of fundamental importance in Rilke's later life. She was unlike anyone else in his life: simple, endearing, charming, happy and capable of giving happiness, unselfish and grateful.

Rilke found rooms in the Bismarckplatz, close to where Benvenuta was living, and she christened the salon the 'Andersen room', something out of a fairy-tale, and ordered a piano to be sent there so that she could play him Beethoven, Bach, Schumann. He was soon at home with Benvenuta's hosts, the Delbrücks, and even in the musical world she provided. They went to hear a recital by Busoni, dining at his house a week later. Benvenuta saw in their greeting the meeting of two worlds:

> Busoni, fiery, witty, positive, a man ready to laugh, naive and superstitious; Rilke, timid, reserved, gravely and anxiously wise, reflective and calm, his sense of humour shining out from time to time. Busoni, who puts from him all that seems faded and *passé*, who is youthful in spirit and lives with the young; Rilke, who evokes the transience of everything, who describes the miserable, the rejected, knowing the sufferings of all creatures but also the supreme happiness of the creative spirit.

Over coffee in the library they discussed Proust and his new novel, which Busoni liked. Rilke found *Du côté de chez Swann* disappointing in parts, though he concluded that the deficiencies were outweighed by the excellence of passages that made the novel not merely diverting, but important. They talked about Busoni's *New Aesthetic of Music,* which so impressed Rilke that he sent it to Kippenberg who issued it in a German translation. And Busoni told Rilke how much he liked 'Lied vom Meer' from the *New Poems,* so Rilke recited it to them. It was a very happy occasion, not the only one in this period when it seemed that Rilke's demons had been laid to rest. He and Benvenuta went to the country together, to the woods and lakes, and his cheeks became sunburned; she could not reconcile this demonstrably human presence with the feeling that he was someone from another world. 'That he had been married, that he had a child, was as unimaginable to me as if an archangel had a human destiny': yet in his presence these contradictions were reconciled.

One evening they went to the Lessing Theatre to see Ibsen's *Brand*. Rilke, exhausted, expounded on the way home his idea that Ibsen had failed to possess the secret of great art because he lacked humility when confronted by fate. Instead of comprehending the divine unpredictable logic of life, he had constantly resorted to reasoning things out. Ibsen had intelligence, imagination, the gift of observation, yet his heart was not great enough, not willing nor generous enough to accept things: consulting cold reason he formed an opinion and thesis which he relentlessly defended. As they said goodnight at the garden door, Rilke regained his calm good humour and said: 'The nicest part of the whole evening was your grey silk dress and the black cape with the golden stars. There was a whole starry sky around you cancelling out all the ugliness.'

There was no doubt that he was in love again. They made plans to visit other cities, and eventually decided to go via Munich, Innsbruck, Zurich and Basle to Paris, which Benvenuta had never seen, and now saw entirely through Rilke's eyes. They arrived on an April evening, and after dining at her hotel walked to Rilke's flat in rue Campagne-Première. 'You will see,' he told her, 'the light here is different from anywhere else; it doesn't seem to fall on houses and bridges and gardens, but it is as if they themselves are illuminated from within.'

Whether she knew it or not, Benvenuta had been given an unrivalled insight not only into his feelings, but also into the smallest events of his existence. She was being allowed to relive his childhood with him, and now Paris was bringing that account up to date. It was as if Rilke could not rest until he had acquainted her with the person he had been at different stages of his life, retraced his whole past with her in order to face a future. That was the time she dreaded, when he might expect a solution to his problems.

He showed her his room: Rodin's table, the desk, the shelves of books, the Rilke arms on the wall, the green shaded lamp on the table; as twilight fell, they could see the cupola of the Invalides rise above the shadowed silent gardens, and through the trees the lights from distant houses. In the stillness Rilke said to Benvenuta:

> Can you feel how I live now? How I live in you, how I am living a
> new life of the spirit since your marvellous arrival, already
> sheltered in you? You must, Benvenuta, you must be able to feel this
> pure raising of my spirit towards you, and the devotion of my whole
> being, wherever you may be.

In the days that followed the conversation often turned to childhood
memories, and Rilke showed her a daguerreotype of his father aged
seventeen, to which he was very attached. He asked Benvenuta
whether childhood could somehow survive within us, disguised from
us by the adult turn towards worldly things, or whether it was a gift
lost before its value could be perceived. They visited Versailles and
Meudon, though Rodin was absent, having gone to see Renoir in the
Midi where each artist was instructing the other. And when Busoni
came to Paris, he invited them to a party which D'Annunzio was also
to attend. Benvenuta did not care to meet him, but Rilke wished to
forearm her for another encounter that he anticipated at Busoni's
concert; if she should see him speaking to a young woman, he asked
that she should be kind. This would be Marthe: Benvenuta concluded
from Rilke's vague description that she was a 'fallen woman'.

'You cannot imagine what potential she has: breadth of thought,
beauty, intelligence, but she will never manage to free herself. Dark
and fatal forces are too strong in her. I can only speak of her real life to
you . . . Even Princess Marie, to whom I have often spoken of Marthe,
thinks I'm in love with her. . . .'

Benvenuta dared not pursue the matter, but she did ask about
Princess Marie, of whom she had never heard before. Rilke told her,
saying that he would like to visit Duino with her, the place where he
had conceived the elegies that he would 'perhaps never finish'. They
did see Marthe at the concert, dressed simply but with great taste;
when Rilke introduced her, Marthe did not take Benvenuta's extended
hand but stammered her thanks and disappeared. Several days later
Marthe explained to Rilke that she had been overjoyed to be so
accepted, but out of respect could not take a lady's hand.

During this time in Paris, Rilke wrote no letters; he was living a new
life of which his friends knew nothing. Benvenuta worried because he
did not seem to be working, they did almost everything together and
his chief pleasure was to listen to her playing, every afternoon or

evening: Handel, especially, and *The Well-Tempered Clavier,* and Beethoven. They went to masses at Notre Dame and at the little Armenian church of St Julien-le-Pauvre, where Rilke seemed to her 'Fra Angelico' among the needy. One evening he fell asleep as she played, and when he eventually woke recounted his dream. He had been waiting in a little station in Russia, and when night came with no sign of a train, he asked an old man what time it would arrive. 'No train comes here'. Rilke went out of the waiting room and saw the tracks deep in grass, themselves covered in rust; he had been forgotten in that infinite solitude. Suddenly, feverishly, he implored Benvenuta not to leave him alone, and she promised to stay until the effects of the nightmare had passed. Rilke realised that he had frightened her, and indeed he was asking for more than momentary consolation.

Benvenuta wrote to her sister Maria:

> You know Rilke, and even if you have only seen him a few times, you know who he is and what he could mean to me.... You did not ask 'What will come of it?' and I have not done so either and perhaps I was right. I never asked any questions, I was happy in his presence, in his noble and pure mind, in his inexhaustible kindness. Every day I was allowed to see him was for me a gift from Heaven. But I thought that when he had to work again, in complete solitude, I would find myself alone, far from him ... Perhaps I would even forbid myself to think of him, but I would always be happy to see him again ...
>
> However, things have happened quite differently. Rainer has asked me if I will agree to stay with him for the rest of our lives.

Rilke was actually contemplating a divorce from Clara in order to marry Benvenuta, who was brought face to face with her feelings. She was not an inexperienced girl, in fact she had been married before to a Viennese psychiatrist, but she panicked now.

> He said that word 'always', that for him is usually so suspect and which he avoids, with a passion and conviction that overwhelmed me. I think I went pale as death, for all the blood rushed to my heart. He took my hands in his and kissed them with such touching consideration that tears came to my eyes. He said I was to say nothing, not a word, not an answer. I was to promise nothing, I was simply to do that which had been

destined 'from all eternity', but that I should know he asked
God each day to make him able to love me in the way
conducive to my happiness. . . . should I feel that it would be
too difficult to bear and share a life such as his, then he asked
me to return to my own life, without promises or thinking of
him, 'simply and boldly'.

Benvenuta, immensely troubled, posed herself a direct question: did
she love him as a woman loves a man with whom she wants to spend
her whole life? And in consequence, enough to want to be the mother
of his children? She reported the answer to her sister: no.

For me he is a voice from God, an immortal soul, Fra
Angelico, everything that is good, sublime, sacred on earth, but
he is not a man. I am indescribably afraid of seeing humanized
the profound, exclusive feeling I have for him . . . And then,
there is something else: somewhere in the world there is a wife
and a child who belong to him.

She did not say these things to Rilke, but read and re-read his letters
and works: at the very moment he was pleading with her, all that he
had written was pleading against him. His wife would be like a sailor's,
she thought, with no conception of the dangers he escaped in order to
return 'sombre, laconic, charged with images and strange feelings of
which he would be incapable of speaking for weeks on end'. In
response, she felt he would require that a woman be absolutely calm,
allowing no fear or anxiety to show, simply to be there 'like the house,
bright during the day and incredibly quiet at night, like the garden . . .'.
Benvenuta recollected his idea of love that he himself admitted to be
impossible: 'If this were love, love infinitely carefree, always rich (and
therefore demanding nothing), yes such a return would surpass
everything, like a blessed death, like a resurrection. But I tell you this:
it is inconceivable.'

Rilke brought her a series of poems with which he was dissatisfied
and seeing that she did not care for them, asked whether he was not
finished as a poet. Benvenuta took her stand: she said she had been
taking up too much of his time, that she also had ten concerts to
prepare for the summer. They agreed not to see each other, but could
not manage such a break. Rilke received an invitation to Duino,
extended also to Benvenuta, and the days until their departure were
spent much as before, although Rilke was often anguished and unwell.

On 22 April they arrived at Duino, greeted by the Princess in evening dress; Benvenuta thought her like a Renaissance patroness of the arts. The days followed a regular course: in the mornings Benvenuta worked at her music, and Rilke in the castle archives; after lunch they rested; around four there was tea, or a trip in the car; in the evenings there was music or reading aloud: the Princess reading *La Vita Nuova* in Italian, or Rilke the poetry of Hölderlin, whom he regarded as one of the greatest lyricists. One evening Benvenuta played Beethoven's Sonata op. 109, scarcely daring to touch the piano on which Liszt had played, and her performance greatly moved Rilke. On another occasion the Princess summoned the Quartetto Triestino in order that they could play together Dvorak's Quintet on the castle terrace. Although Rilke's physical health improved under this benign régime, he became quieter, slept later, seemed to have abandoned all work. Benvenuta sensed that they were drifting apart, a separation marked by one episode. Rilke received some drawings of dolls which Benvenuta found hideous, while he considered them movingly beautiful. Determined to make her understand his point of view, Rilke pulled out his essay 'Dolls' — on the puppets of Lotte Pritzel — which had been published in *Weisse Blätter* in March, and began to read it:

> ... dragged through the changing emotions of the day, basking in each; like a dog made an accessory after the fact, an accomplice, but unlike it not accepting and forgetting, a double burden; initiated into the first nameless experiences of their owners, lying in their earliest uncanny loneliness as if in empty rooms, as though it were only a question of exploiting the new space with all their limbs; hauled off to cradles, hidden in the heavy folds of illness, appearing in dreams, a party to the events of nights of fever: thus were these dolls. They themselves made no effort at all but lay at the edge of childhood sleep, at the most filled with rudimentary thoughts of falling; letting themselves be dreamed; as, during the day, they were accustomed to being lived inexhaustibly by alien forces.

He asked whether he should continue and Benvenuta, hoping for some consoling resolution, said he should.

> When one considers how grateful things are normally for tenderness, how they recover with its aid, yes, how even the most merciless usage (provided that one loves them) affects them only as a consuming caress, under which they may become giddy but, as it

were, take heart... and if one remembers the subtle beauty certain things can acquire by being caught up in the warp of human existence... I pass over the intimate, touching, dreaming solitude of many things that have impressed me in their gentle cohabitation with the human; I should like to mention in passing a few simple ones: a sewing-case, a spinning wheel, a domestic loom, a bride's glove, a cup, the binding and pages of a bible; not to mention the great will of a hammer, the surrender of a violin, the good-natured eagerness of a pair of horn-rimmed spectacles, yes if you throw on the table that card game with which you had often had success, then you will see it surrounded by melancholy hopes and long since overtaken by other events. If one could make all this actual, and at the same time, under a heap of things one regarded most sympathetically, one found a doll: it would almost anger us by its terrible, its gross lack of memory; the hatred which, unconsciously, was always part of our relationship to it, would appear; unmasked, it would lie there before us, as the horrible foreign body on which we had lavished our purest warmth; like a drowned corpse, lightly veiled, which was borne and carried on the flood of our tenderness, until we had dried again and had forgotten it in some bush.

While admiring his prose, Benvenuta listened with growing uneasiness. Could he possibly be making reference to her own situation? She dreaded this Rilke, either too innocent or too cruel.

Did we not stand in front of it, trembling with rage, wanting to know, item by item, why it wanted our warmth... Then it kept silent, not because it felt superior to us, but because that was its usual mode of expression, because it was made of absolutely useless, unaccountable material, it was silent... in a world where destiny and God Himself had become notable because of the silence they kept obstinately...
I remember having seen somewhere, in a distant Russian estate, an old doll in the children's hands, inherited, which the whole family resembled...
And in the end no one held you, and you were stepped on...

Benvenuta suddenly felt she would have to weep without stopping, she could not bear to hear any more:

... I know I am stupid and childish, and I don't know why your hatred of dolls should so affect me, after all it is your hatred and not mine — but I cannot share it. I find it frightening; it means... the destruction of the simplest and most innocent feelings and joys. Do you understand?

She turned to play the piano; when she had finished the Bach fugue and looked around, Rilke had gone.

In the days that succeeded, he became increasingly fond of listening to Chopin, especially the Funeral March whose tragedy seemed that of his own life. Although Benvenuta tried to combat this sense of tragedy, it was confirmed for her one evening when he read the *Elegies*. She had seen his enthusiasm, his humour, his joy submerged in a suffering she felt she could not lighten. Their visit drew to a close, the Princess having decided to stay with friends in Venice; Rilke wavered between going and staying, joining the Princess or travelling with Benvenuta. The day before they left they could not go out for the rain which ploughed up the garden. For an hour Benvenuta played to the Princess and Rilke, who seemed downcast and laconic. When they were alone she discovered that he had received a letter from his mother, describing various devotional exercises in which she had taken part, the saints to whom she commended the care of his soul; admonishing him not to be 'lukewarm in displaying the true piety of the ardent Catholic', and asking him to send another parcel of his gloves, which she claimed the exclusive privilege of washing. Handing back the letter in silence, Benvenuta saw him stroke the sheets as if in forgiveness of the stranger 'who by chance brought me into the world'. At night Rilke read them some poems by Stefan George, and when they retired the Princess embraced Benvenuta with particular affection. The older woman had no doubt warned her against taking on 'Dr Serafico'.

In the early morning, as Benvenuta was putting the last things in her bag, Rilke knocked and asked to come in for a moment. He brought her the inkwell he had used when writing *Malte,* which she had seen on his desk in Paris and admired, saying that it would be in better and more beautiful hands with her. There was one thing he wanted to say, staring out at the landscape still wrapped in mist:

I once told you I went from your kindness into your patience, as if from one room into another: as though I had the right to go everywhere.... But I shall never be able to tell you what you have done for me.... And what have I done? I have put the heavy stone of my pain over your joy, my withering presence next to your confidence and disappointed it. I have taken your flowers into my hands and they have faded. I thought I could offer you my life, but it is cursed. . . . Can you forgive me all that?

She told him how glad she had been to share part of his life, the sorrow as well as the joy, and he was grateful that she had something to give, even then. When she went downstairs the Princess bundled her into a car, remarking that it was lucky that 'our Serafico' had overslept and missed them. Benvenuta said nothing.

The Princess went to her flat in Venice, Benvenuta to the Hotel Bristol. Sitting out on the terrace after mass on Sunday, she looked up at a gondolier's call and saw Rilke waving at her from the gondola. For a moment she thought everything would be all right; he promised to show her 'his' Venice in the afternoon when he had rested, but would not go with her to the Princess's. At lunch Benvenuta met the young Titi Taxis-Metternich, with whom she became good friends, and the Baron Franchetti, owner of the Ca d'Oro, whom the Princess considered the last *nobile* of Venice. On her return, Benvenuta found Rilke so recovered and merry that the previous few days seemed like a bad dream.

During the next week they walked all over Venice, and went for tea one afternoon at the Ca d'Oro, where the Baron lived simply in two rooms. He showed them the treasures of the house — a Mantegna, a Carpaccio, a Venus by Titian, a series of portraits by Tintoretto — and said that he intended donating the entire house to Venice 'in gratitude for having been born and lived here'. Amidst all this loveliness and ease, Rilke and Benvenuta knew that separation was ahead though neither mentioned it. Only once, when Rilke said he thought he would go to Assisi, did he look at her inquiringly.

'I hope with all my heart that your days there may be blessed with quiet and work,' she replied.

She thought his face became a shade paler as he leaned forward to ask: 'And you?'

'I shall go to Maria's,' she said, turning away to hide her tears.

'Don't be afraid, dear child, don't be afraid. I am returning to the suffering I have never renounced. Everything is as it must be, you are right, and it's as well this way.'

Benvenuta's decision was supported by Princess Marie, who advised her not to devote herself to the life of constant movement that music entailed, but to find someone on whom she could rely for love and strength, someone to lead her 'into light not into sorrow'. Rilke, said the Princess, was not such a man:

> You have great power over him — and you perhaps do not know how much he loves you — but his demon also has great power; he is constantly hesitating between you and his work and he often seems disillusioned and despondent, because you have your own personality, full of vitality, and are not the docile creature with no will of her own that he perhaps needs.... you would shatter your own life without being any help to him. His duty is to be alone, his sacrifice is suffering, which will raise him to new and great creativity, believe me.

Even at this stage, Benvenuta was unsure whether she should accept the insidious doctrine of the necessity of sorrow, which for Rilke had been summed up by Kassner: 'From inwardness to greatness there is only one way, sacrifice'. On their last evening together, they sat up until dawn talking, and she found she could say to him everything she had been storing up. They kissed for the first and last time when he took leave of her at the hotel, but she saw him again from the train window. Just as the train began to move Rilke reached out suddenly for her hand, then each was alone.

He could not stay in Venice, and left the next day for Assisi, where he spent twelve days before going on to Milan, reaching Paris on 25 May. On 8 June he resumed his correspondence with Lou Andreas-Salomé, in despair and self-condemnation. If in the past he had blamed other people for the failure of his attempts 'to obtain a human and natural foothold in life', he had now come to realise that even the most loving of hearts could not sustain him, would be stripped of its joy by him.

> In the end something will have been learnt, — at present of course I realize only this: that once more I was not able to fulfil a pure and pious duty which life again presented to me, guilelessly, forgivingly, as though it had not had any ill experience of me. Now it is clear that this time too I have failed my exam and will not be moved up, but must sit still for another year in the same agonizing class and... be given those same words on the blackboard whose accents I thought I had learned from the very bottom of my heart.

On 20 June he sent her a poem he had written that morning, 'because I involuntarily called it "Turning" [*Wendung*], and because it represents the turning that *must* come if I am to live...'. Its epigraph was Kassner's sentence, and it read in part:

> Gazing, how long?
> For how long, the inward sacrifice,
> and the pleading glance?
>
> When, waiting, he sat abroad: the busy
> room of the hotel, turned away
> grumbling, about him, and in the avoided mirror
> again, the room
> and later from the tortured bed
> again:
> then the air deliberated
> incredibly deliberated
> over his susceptible heart,
> over the heart susceptible still
> through the painful wasted body;
> deliberated and judged
> that it lacked love.
>
> (And refused further consecration.)
>
> For there is a limit to gazing, you see,
> and the over-observed world
> desires to advance in love.
>
> The work of vision is over.
> Do heart-work now
> at the images in you, the trapped: for you
> overcame them, but now you know them no more.
> See, man within, the woman within,
> that only now conquered creature
> never yet loved, though won
> from a thousand natures.
>
> Schauend wie lang?
> Seit wie lange schon innig entbehrend,
> flehend im Grunde des Blicks?

Wenn er, ein Wartender, sass in der Fremde; des Gasthofs
zerstreutes, abgewendetes Zimmer
mürrisch um sich, und im vermiedenen Spiegel
wieder das Zimmer,
und später vom quälenden Bett aus
wieder:
da beriets in der Luft,
unfassbar beriet es
über sein fühlbares Herz,
über sein durch den schmerzhaft verschütteten Körper
dennoch fühlbares Herz
beriet es und richtete:
dass es der Liebe nicht habe.

(Und verwehrte ihm weitere Weihen.)

Denn des Anschauns, siehe, ist eine Grenze.
Und die geschautere Welt
will in der Liebe gedeihn.

Werk des Gesichts ist getan,
tue nun Herz-Werk
an den Bildern in dir, jenen gefangenen; denn du
überwältigtest sie: aber nun kennst du sie nicht.
Siehe, innerer Mann, dein inneres Mädchen,
dieses errungene aus
tausend Naturen, dieses
erst nur errungene, nie
noch geliebte Geschöpf.

Silent observation and experience should one day be made fruitful, but
only by recognizing the 'woman', the feminine element in man's
nature which enabled love.

In July he was writing to Benvenuta that he hoped to begin work
again on the *Elegies,* and seemed oblivious to any hints of war. She did
not reply, but considered the meaning of sacrifice for him, recalling
what he had once said when he came across the word in a newspaper,
defining sacrifice as 'the firm and unqualified determination of a man
to attain his purest inner potential':

Generally, the evil and superficially Christian use of the word
makes it suspect to me, and what it meant in its ancient, fiery sense,
none of us has understood. And yet there it lies: 'The way from
inwardness to greatness lies through sacrifice'. That went right
through me. Like a dagger sharpened against one and carried by an
assassin all year under his cloak, never out of the hand waiting to
strike, just as such a dagger leaps up and is plunged into the actual
chest, so that struck me. Yes, that was it: I had the intensity, I
possessed it to a high degree, but I possessed only that. For my work
to be realized the other was necessary: greatness. Thus the bridge
was defined: where was my sacrifice?

She wondered whether he had resolved the question.

There seemed to have been plenty of sacrifices: of home and of
security, of the hope of 'success', perhaps of Paula and now of
Benvenuta; but importantly they lay in his state of mind. For Rilke, his
final acceptance of life was the sacrifice that counted.

XII

Pain in Action

In July 1914, knowing what a political innocent Rilke was, Lou Andreas-Salomé sent him an invitation to come and visit her. Had he stayed in Paris, he would certainly have been interned when war broke out.

He went on to visit the Kippenbergs in Leipzig again. High trees from the neighbour's land made the garden like a park, where Rilke sat out in the sunshine to read Gundolf's translation of Shakespeare and his own Egyptian poems. They went back to Weimar and saw over Goethe's house. Rilke did not seem to Frau Kippenberg particularly attracted to Goethe, but he was extremely interested in one poem in the Archives, *Wenn du im Tanze dich regst,* which he said had been written down in a flow of inspiration, as he could tell from the words and rhythm.

Sometimes he talked to Frau Kippenberg about his aesthetic ideas, and how the world of things was 'withdrawn from the world of becoming, and had become being', one of his favourite phrases. He said, as he had once written to Clara, that it was becoming increasingly difficult to find in the external world equivalents for the workings of the spirit. The problem of action was the core of his preoccupation here. He accepted that action was becoming ineluctably impossible, and thought that this was in the order of things, since the whole of reality became invisible in the process of time. 'The nearer one approaches pure art, the more purpose falls away from the thing, until it stands there alone, to fulfil itself.'

The wonderful summer went on, the summer of decay. In the mornings and evenings he helped Frau Kippenberg to water the flowers, and indoors at night, with the curtains drawn and the candles lit, he read aloud the first two *Duino Elegies.* Frau Kippenberg has described the effect of the verses as of the onset of apocalyptic riders. Light and dark fought with each other; the poems were in flames; roses shone through the room. An unusually receptive woman, she heard in his strange lines the massing of powerful, unearthly forces that seemed to herald destruction, a kind of celestial cavalry. On hearing the news of the declaration of war, Rilke stood up, fetched his Bible and sat down to read about the prophet Elijah. The following day he left for Munich, and took his leave of the Kippenbergs amid a swirl of field-grey uniforms and girls carrying flowers. The soldiers intended to be back by Christmas: like them, he thought they were setting out on little more than an exercise. Had the war not intervened, there might have been a chance of his hearing from Benvenuta, perhaps even seeing her again. As Frau Kippenberg recorded, Rilke never got over the fact that the war had happened at all.

At first he was seized by something of the same feeling of social solidarity as poets in England experienced, and began his five hymns to the war-god. The God who he thought had deserted him was suddenly there, in terrifying form it is true, nevertheless present. The hymns had their own splendour, undoubtedly influenced by Rilke's reading of Hölderlin and his concept of the poet-prophet empowered to address his people publicly, though he was none too happy with the poems.

> Godhead at last! And we who so often failed
> to hold fast to the peaceful god are suddenly seized by the war-god,
> hurling his brand: while over the heart rich with home
> the heavens scream, blood-red, where thundering he dwells.

> Endlich ein Gott. Da wir den friedlichen oft
> nicht mehr ergriffen, ergreift uns plötzlich der Schlacht-Gott,
> schleudert den Brand: und über dem Herzen voll Heimat
> schreit, den er donnernd bewohnt, sein rötlicher Himmel.

There were magnificent passages, as in the third hymn where Rilke sings the god:

> Like some volcanic peak he lay to the westward. Sometimes
> flaming. Sometimes asmoke. Sorrowing and godlike.
> Only perhaps some district near to his borders
> would quake. But we raised aloft our undamaged lyres
> to others . . .

> Wie ein vulkanischer Berg lag er im Weiten. Manchmal
> flammend. Manchmal im Rauch. Traurig und göttlich.

Nur eine nahe vielleicht, ihm anliegende Ortschaft
bebte. Wir aber hoben die heile
Leyer anderen zu...

For once Rilke's 'I' was stilled, without causing him overanxiety.
Better, he seemed to think, a god like that than none at all, not realizing
that was what the war would reveal: none at all, nihilism gone mad. It
was not the petty being cast aside, as he imagined, but all that was
brave, civilised and decent. It was not a volcano erupting with
eloquence and majesty, not a spectacle, but a pagan sacrifice, a
primitive, fearful, greedy sacrifice for base ends.

Rilke's elation, however, was a temporary aberration. By the end of
August his war-god was mute. He had become aware that the loss of
identity the war involved was a positive danger if it meant merging
with the mass and the surrender of human responsibility to the State.
On 4 October he wrote to Prince Alexander von Thurn und Taxis: '...
one can hardly hear oneself live; it is as if one were standing day and
night by the most thunderous waterfall...'.

On the day that war broke out Benvenuta was giving a concert at
Lake Garda. She had no idea where Rilke was but tried to send a
telegram to Paris, only to be informed that the frontiers were closed. A
few weeks elapsed before she had a letter from him, written from the
Isartal:

> But believe me, faced by these immense events my pen has
> been completely mute. Who exists? Who feels himself living,
> thinking, being? Is this still me? I often ask myself. Are we the
> same people? No, we have all been thrust out forcibly into a
> strange world, which has nothing in common with the one that
> went before except that it is incomprehensible, but in a new
> way, frightening and fatal.

He was still hoping to find somewhere quiet in which he might be able
to work, probably in Munich. Clara had offered him the use of her flat,
but he had declined, saying that his doctor had recommended his going
to the country. When he returned, Rilke lived in various pensions; in
fact during July 1914-June 1919 he changed address at least twenty-
eight times. Forced back on himself more and more, he read widely:
Yeats, Verhaeren, Büchner; Werfel, whom he much admired;
Montaigne, the later works of Strindberg and above all, Hölderlin.

In the autumn Benvenuta gave a concert in Munich, hesitating as to seeing the poet or not. Just as she was trying to rid herself of an importunate agent, there was a knock at the door of her room: a beautifully-timed visit from Rilke. It was strange that he should come just then but, he said mischievously, that was what he was for. She thought he seemed quieter and more collected, also healthier; and seeing Benvenuta did something to restore his *joie de vivre*. He was living fairly quietly, though he frequented the salon of Hugo Bruckmann, the great publisher, and his wife, née Princess Cantacuzène, who collected together the intellectual, artistic and musical élite of Munich. Rilke did not mention his own work, but often talked to Benvenuta about Goethe, whom he had discovered as it were only in the last couple of years, and whom he now found 'humanly touching'. Their meetings were happy, and they looked forward to seeing each other again in Berlin, where Benvenuta would be playing in military hospitals.

In the interval, his letters again revealed disquiet. When Benvenuta asked why he did not preserve his solitude as in Paris, Rilke replied that there no one had come to see him, 'But here. . . . And the worst is that I cannot say no'. He had put much of his subtle art into human relations, and that made him immensely attractive. His life in Berlin, from November to January 1915, was a whirl of social activity. Financiers were falling over themselves to invite him to tea, lunch, the theatre; he was consulted about buying pictures, invited to dancers' débuts, or to hear a new star at the opera. He did find time to accompany Benvenuta to the Egyptian Museum in order to see the head of Amenophis IV, about which he had written to her before they ever met. Now she appreciated his remark: 'Could one not turn aside from a night of stars to find the same law blossoming in this face?' Egypt had captivated him more than he knew.

Later Benvenuta gave a benefit concert at which Rilke was present; he divined that she was playing for him, and said as they parted at her gate: 'I cannot thank you enough for your music. Perhaps tonight someone very great and far-off will express what I cannot, because it lies too deep in me.' Puzzling over his words, she went to her room, switched on the light, only to find on the table a replica of the head of Amenophis together with a garland of red roses.

It was to be their last happy encounter. Benvenuta did not see him again until a year later, in Munich. By then he was seldom alone, often with someone who wanted to be rescued or consoled. Rilke told her of a painter whom he saw frequently and who required his help, Lou

Albert-Lasard, who years before had spoken of him as 'an adventurer'. He never mentioned his work; his solitary pleasure was to go to art exhibitions or to the Pinakothek, where he lingered over the works of El Greco and Brueghel. Benvenuta and Rilke corresponded, but one of the most arid periods of his life had begun, relieved by an occasional trip to the country, where he appeared in pensions and boarding-houses he had never frequented before. He had come to the conclusion, as he told Frau Kippenberg, that it was his fate 'to have no fate'. With a friend he called on a local clairvoyante, who put her hands over her eyes and cried, 'Terrible, terrible; never have I seen anything like it!' She claimed that the greatest power she had ever encountered emanated from Rilke.

Yet in some senses his luck held. At the beginning of the war a stranger left Rilke 20,000 kronen in his will, which Rilke accepted 'as he did the unicorn, as an act of faith'. He submitted proposals for its expenditure to Kippenberg, which included buying clothes to replace those left behind in Paris, and paying off debts. There was even a suggestion that he might return to university studies. In early 1915 there was another windfall: an anonymous donor — whom we now know to have been Ludwig Wittgenstein — produced a substantial amount of money for the benefit of poets, and Trakl and Rilke were chosen as the recipients. That spring he wrote to Herta Koenig, more or less asking for the use of her flat when she went to the country, which was granted him. From there Rilke wrote to Thankmar von Münchhausen on 28 June:

> ... the fact that so much greatness is displayed and maintained can hardly lessen the pain of knowing that this chaos, this ineffectual blundering... this unmitigated catastrophe was actually *necessary* to extort proofs of courageousness, devotion and grandeur. Whereas *we,* the arts, the theatre, aroused nothing in these selfsame people, brought nothing to the top, could change nobody. What else is our function but to present grounds for change, true and broad and free? Have we done this so badly, so half-heartedly, so unconvinced and unconvincing?
>
> ... for the time being I sit in the flat of some acquaintances... with the loveliest of all Picassos (the *Saltimbanques*) in which there is so much of Paris I sometimes forget.

He lived with the Picasso for nearly four months, and his contemplation of it was vital for the composition of the fifth *Elegy*. There were still too many demands on his time, however, and he wrote to Princess Marie that he knew he ought to leave Munich if he were to work at all.

> My position has, so to speak, been clarified by my learning
> yesterday that all my property in Paris ... has really been lost:
> the entire contents of my flat were auctioned in April! You
> know that I do not take this hard, I have long been disposed to
> regard all the things that have congregated round me for the
> last twelve years in Paris as the effects of the late Malte
> Laurids Brigge ... [but] now that I know everything has gone a
> strange fear stirs in me, that it might be possible suddenly to be
> seized by the memory of a lost object that is absolutely
> indispensable ... with annihilation we have the profoundest and
> most absolute affinities, but there is something particularly
> rueful about losing one's possessions, no matter how peculiar
> they are, to strangers.
>   ... it is, I know, a question of winning an *inner* resting-place;
> only, an impressionable person like me takes it for granted that
> the right conditions outside will help the inner ones. *Je suis un*
> *enfant qui ne voudrait autour que des enfances toujours plus*
> *adultes.*   (August 1915)

Perhaps a few days earlier he had written to her about his outburst to Marthe, years before, which he had then thought of only with regard to his personal fortunes, but now saw as having a general validity: '*Marthe, il n'y aura devant moi que des désastres, des terreurs, des angoisses indicibles: c'est avec vous que finissent les bontés de ma vie.*'

> Only now do I see that this was precisely how the few mighty
> old men went about, Tolstoy and Cézanne, uttering threats and
> warnings, like the prophets of an ancient order about to be
> broken — an order they did not wish to see broken and live.
> Whatever comes, the worst is that a certain innocence of life in
> which we grew up will never again be there for any of
> us.   (2 August)

On leaving the Koenigs', Rilke was offered refuge in Munich by Renée Alberti, wife of a Counsellor to the Legation. The prospect of being reasonably settled again helped him to devote time to his work.

At the end of October he had rather despaired of being able to write at the required pitch, writing of Toledo to Ellen Delp on the 27th:

> ... for there the outward things themselves — tower, mountain, bridge — instantly possessed the unparalleled, unsurpassable intensity of the inner equivalents through which one would have wished to portray them. Appearance and vision everywhere merged in the object, in each a whole interior world was revealed, as though an angel who encompassed all space were blind and gazing into himself. This, a world no longer seen from the standpoint of people, but *in* the angel, is perhaps my real task, at least all my previous endeavours would be united in it ...

For this he needed to be 'sheltered and resolute', which he must have felt in November as he composed the fourth *Elegy* on the 22nd and 23rd. On the 24th he was pronounced fit for military service, and ordered to report for service with the last infantry reserve, the *Landsturm,* at Turnau on January 4th. As he later recounted to Kippenberg (15 February, 1916):

> ... I was making rapid progress in my work and was in the midst of a veritable siege: several remarkable poems, the elegies as well, everything was rising with a rush, and the collection of Michaelangelo poems increasing daily ... Never have I written such strong, accurate and clean-cut translations. I believed myself to be standing on the verge of the freest vision, when the thick grey military cloth blotted everything out.

Rilke's service in the *Landsturm* was not brilliant. He did approximately three weeks drill, by which time he was on the verge of collapse. Then he was transferred to Vienna to serve in the Military Records Office. There his hours were from nine to three, after which he would eat and go home by tram to the Park Hotel, Hietzing, feeling incapable of doing any real work in the evenings. His duties were called by others *Heldenfrisieren,* hero-building. Rilke was supposed to write up selected reports that came in from the front, dealing with particular deeds of daring or heroism, tidying them up for the public, or in the German phrase, 'giving the heroes a hair-cut'. It was an appropriate task for the author of the *Cornet* — sales of which had shot up to a quarter of a million — if not entirely congenial. Rilke called his work *Dichtdienst,* writing duty, like sentry-duty, telling Kippenberg:

'They do not know what to do with me and are keeping me in the prolonged idleness that constitutes one of the great military experiences.'

Frau Schalk, an Austrian actress and friend of Hofmannsthal, met him at this time and remembered his being most resentful of the army, using a phrase to her which he might have heard in the Military Academy: *'All diesen Schmutz in die Augen schmieren zu lassen, ist schrecklich'* — 'To have all that filth rubbed in one's eyes...'. On the whole, however, Rilke was treated very well by the Austrian authorities. When he refused to compile direct propaganda, they declared themselves satisfied if he would 'go through the motions', which in the end entailed ruling straight lines on the pay-sheets. In March Rilke moved to a flat in Viktorgasse placed at his disposal by Princess Marie, who took him about. Meanwhile Frau Kippenberg had been making representations to the authorities for his release, and on 9 June 1916 he was officially demobilized. He went to the Hotel Stelzer at Rodaun, near Vienna, where he was joined by Loulou Albert-Lasard, who painted his portrait.

In her memoir Benvenuta records their last meeting, which occurred in this period: Rilke had stopped writing to her after his call-up. Walking down a crowded street in the centre of Vienna, she saw him approaching with a woman on his arm, a woman heavily made-up and limping. Rilke's eyes blazed when he suddenly glimpsed Benvenuta; his companion said something to him in obvious mockery, he ducked his head and they went on. His cutting her dead on the street seemed to kill something for Benvenuta. Rilke was still tending to swing between the roles of comforter and comforted: was it that he was ashamed to reveal to Benvenuta his dependence on someone he had portrayed as dependent on him? Perhaps the Lou Albert-Lasard who had called him 'an adventurer' had a hold over him because she had no illusions; that would be in keeping with the 'mocking expression' Benvenuta detected on her face.

However that may be, it took Rilke a long time to settle down again. He had the opportunity of seeing his family more often than before, and when in Munich saw them once a week without apparent strain. They moved to Fischerhude near Bremen, and on one occasion Rilke spent the day looking after Ruth in Munich before she caught the train home. Yet like his own panther he began to pace the length of his cage; as late as 15 April 1917 he could still attribute this restlessness to the 'Vienna interruption', in a letter to Kippenberg:

Its fatal similarity with that hardest stratum of my life, the
military academy, has done the same kind of thing to me ... as
would happen to a tree, if it found itself temporarily turned
upside down, its crown in the refractory and hostile earth from
which a tree-generation ago it had thrust itself up into the
light, after the most incredible efforts. To which must be added
the fact that this crown, at the moment when it was buried,
was full of new sap and ready to blossom and bear fruit as it
had not done for years.

In November he was ready to write Clara a birthday letter when he
heard the news of Rodin's death, by which he was deeply depressed.
They had not been in contact for years, and in normal circumstances
Rilke thought he might have been reconciled to the death, but not in
the general chaos: '... behind the unnatural and terrible ramparts of
the war these familiar known figures sink away from us, who can tell
where? — Verhaeren, Rodin, — the great wise friends, their death
becomes blurred and unrecognisable...' (19 November, 1917). Of
course Rilke had also lost friends who had been drafted: George Trakl,
one of the finest young German poets, committed suicide while
serving on the Eastern Front in 1914; Alfred Heymel died of
consumption the same year. Rilke had written to Benvenuta that,
though it was difficult to tell if his verses were inspired by the
confusion of the world, or whether his own confusion had been
projected on to the world, Heymel was well worth reading; he
travelled to Berlin to be with the young poet in his last hours. He
wrote to Hans Carossa soon after the harrowing event, 'Do you have
to assist at *such* deaths?' Nevertheless he exposed himself to similar
impressions, and Carossa seeing him on such an occasion said that the
extinguished light in Rilke's face struck him as had a great bird's dying.
Norbert von Hellingrath, who had worked on the authoritative
edition of Hölderlin's poems and brought them to Rilke's attention,
died before Verdun on 14 December 1916. Rilke felt that he had had
lead poured over him, he said, so numb were all his feelings and listless
his reactions.

This was his state when he met the young poet and soldier Bernhard
von der Marwitz at a literary party in Berlin in October 1917, who was
immensely impressed by 'the great "Hyperion" Rilke'. Von der
Marwitz prevailed upon him to write to him at the front, which Rilke
was loath to do. He felt unable to provide the one thing that might be

useful in letters from home: a sense of spiritual continuity. He inveighed against the part civilians were expected to play amidst the terrible events, reading the newspapers:

> ... letting yourself be stuffed full of the fictitious, bogus events that are amassed daily, so that in the end you can conceive of pain and anxiety only in the version which the papers impose upon everything. Terrible though the war is in itself, it seems to me still more terrible that its pressure has nowhere contributed to make man more recognizably human, to urge them towards God, either as individuals or in the mass, which was the effect of great disasters in earlier times. On the plane which has meanwhile developed, and on which the newspapers are expert at giving an unscrupulous cross-section of all these events ... a continual cancelling-out of all tension takes place, and humanity is taught to accept a world of news instead of reality ...   (9 March 1918)

Von der Marwitz replied in August with a letter Rilke later described as 'glorious', but he delayed his own response, only to learn that the soldier had died of wounds on 8 September. In great grief he wrote to Joachim von Winterfeldt-Menkin that he had 'regarded this friendship as an untouched legacy whose future riches seemed all the more precious because men have so seldom essayed an intimate attachment with me' (16 September). A week later he sent a letter in the same vein to Marie von Bunsen:

> Two cherished young friends were snatched from me in August and September by the war, friends whom I lament infinitely in the interests of the hoped-for future, — young Keyserlingk and that rare and excellent young Marwitz of Friedersdorf, whom perhaps you also knew. I was on the point of gaining his love. ...

If the war was now drawing to its close, Rilke knew there was no real promise of peace. He wrote to Clara on 7 November: '... at each pause in the march of what has at last come, one's heart stands still, as if the future, still struggling on foot through the tumult, might fall or turn back once more.'

XIII

The Broken Order

The best picture of the poet during the Munich period after his demobilization is given by Elizabeth Schmidt-Pauli in her memoir, *Rainer Maria Rilke, ein Gedenkbuch*. She was one of the many women friends who surrounded him at this time, such as Isabella Hilbert, who invited him to Burghausen in the winter of 1916; Countess Dietrichstein, Marietta Countess of Nordeck-Rabenau, Elizabeth Countess of Schenk-Schweinsberg. He relied on such women's sympathy and support, and in return offered some inspiration and consolation during the most difficult years of the war and afterwards. One day Elizabeth Schmidt-Pauli asked him why he did not put more of his personal feelings into his poetry. In reply he pointed to a tree:

> Look, I should like so to express this tree that only the tree is there, just as it is — with nothing of Rilke in it at all. My poem 'The Ball' was successful in this way. It was expressive only of pure movement. You see, somewhere deep in us must lie the point at which we know everything, can do everything, are everything, and stand in unity with everything. We should take it very seriously and descend into our depths, in order to find the spot.

He was still trying vainly to achieve some sort of inner calm. All through the war he had been the centre of a fashionable circle in Munich, largely aristocratic and female; with the prolongation of hostilities he saw that circle thinning. The web he had spun again and again over the abyss was broken. Rilke found it more and more difficult to dispense comfort and advice, partly because people demanded more; partly became he himself was older and unwilling to dissipate energies that might be used for work; but mainly because the social circumstances to which he had become accustomed were now being rent asunder. As a poet he saw and admitted the necessity for a transformation of society; as a man he trembled for the effects upon

121

himself and those around him. When writing to Marie von Bunsen, Rilke had expressed a longing

> for people through whom the past, in all its great outlines, remains linked to us: for at present the more daring and bold our conception of the future is, the more dependent it will be on whether development takes place in line with the deepest tradition and inspired by it, and not by its negation.

By late 1918 Rilke was at least comfortably settled in Munich, with a flat in the Ainmillerstrasse and a good housekeeper, Rosa, who did her best to keep visitors at bay. There were no pictures on the walls, as they tended to distract him, but flowers everywhere. The material circumstances for work were encouraging, the spirit to do so was lacking. When Rilke resumed writing letters, they were all on the same theme:

> What is one to write, when all one touches is unknowable, unutterable, and when nothing belongs to one any longer, no feelings and no hope; when a monstrous store of suffering and despair and sacrifice and human need deriving from I know not where, is being consumed on an immense scale, as though it were all being kept together somewhere and there was nothing for the individual? The scale of the human heart no longer applies and yet it was once the unit of the earth, and of Heaven, and of all heights and depths.

At the beginning it was not really the God of war he had hymned, but the possibility within the framework of the war of founding a new age on earth, and of changing human nature. As he had written in the fifth hymn: 'Do not imitate / What has gone before, and was once. Test / To see if you are not pain. Pain in action' ('Ahmt nicht / Früherem nach, Einstigem. Prüfet, / ob ihr nicht Schmerz seid. Handelnder Schmerz.'). The longer the war lasted, the more clearly he saw the impossibility of such hopes being realised and became silent except for the outcries in his letters. Rilke wrote to Ellen Delp on 10 October 1915:

> Can no one stop or arrest it? Why do not two or three or five or ten stand together and shout: Enough! and be shot and at least have given their lives for the idea that we have had enough? The others out there are dying only in order that it

should go on and on and on, and that there should be no end to destruction. Why is there no one who *will* not stand it any more, who refuses to bear it.... Am I in error, or are there not many who would cry out? If not, then I do not know humanity, and am not human, and have nothing in common with humanity.

Towards the end of the war, in Munich, Rilke was able to observe just such manifestations of a common humanity. There were huge gatherings in beer-halls, or outdoors, almost every night; Rilke reported to Clara on a meeting in November addressed by Max Weber. One young worker stood up to ask why the offer of an armistice had not been made directly:

> '... *we* are the people who ought to have done it, not these gentlemen at the top; if we could get hold of a radio station and speak as common people to the common people over there, peace would come at once.' I cannot say it half as well as he did... 'Here, these professors, they can speak French, they'll help us to say it properly...' Such moments are wonderful, there have been all too few of them here in Germany, where only intransigence found words, or submission which in its way is only a participation in violence by the oppressed.
>
> (7 November 1918)

On the day he wrote, 120,000 people gathered on the Theresienwiese and a council of soldiers, peasants and workers was set up with Kurt Eisner as the first President. Rilke wrote in a postscript: 'Up to now all seems quiet and you cannot do otherwise than admit that the times are right for trying to take big steps...'.

Accompanying Elizabeth Schmidt-Pauli home from a similar meeting, he heard machine-gun fire in the town. Bullets were spattering the streets they knew so well. It grew dark; they stopped in a doorway and Elizabeth began to weep. Rilke comforted her, saying that such things were to be expected when there were great changes in the air.

After the short-lived Bavarian Soviet Republic, Rilke was appalled by the outbreak of the White Terror. The fighting in the town seemed not to have the remotest connection with their lives. One morning at five soldiers arrived to search Rilke's rooms: he was suspected of being a Bolshevik. Asked if he believed in any particular form of politics, he replied that he was a poet, only to be met with much the same mockery as in military school. The revolution, he wrote to a friend, had been seized by an opportunist and sceptical minority; it had neither youth nor fire. After four years' blood-letting, a revolution — defined idiosyncratically as 'the conquest of abuses in favour of the deepest tradition, and against political dilettantism' — was not possible. Rilke's lack of faith in political solutions was due to the fact that for him the only real revolution was concerned with human nature, and he could not accept that this could be accomplished from the outside. Meanwhile his daughter Ruth's conception of the revolution led her to abandon school for the life of a hard-working peasant, and Rilke recounted this to Elisabeth von der Heydt with approval: '... it was sheer bliss for her, she said, to be *needed* in that little place of hers, — and since there was not exactly a superfluity of happy people just now, she would insist all the more on having her own way. Could anything be better?' (20 March 1919).

Rilke informed friends that he was waiting for some 'sign' as to what he should he do next. He worked on his Michelangelo translations and longed to leave Munich, to leave Germany altogether: rescue came in the form of an invitation to give lectures in Switzerland; a visa was obtained for that purpose and offers of hospitality began to arrive. Rilke thought that an intellectual could not take sides in the complicated political struggle going on in Germany; it was his part to prepare the almost unnoticed changes of heart that were necessary, and that work Rilke could not do in Munich:

> There was an unbearable tension everywhere. For behind all
> the revolution and noise and malevolent pressure there was no
> desire for real change and renewal. Spiritual man must always
> oppose and deny revolutions, since he knows how long it takes
> to make changes of lasting value; how casual and almost
> invisible they are; and how nature, in its work of creation,
> hardly ever allows violent methods to be used.

In the years 1917 and 1918 he had written only three poems.

He packed his things carefully, locking away private papers, daily diaries and manuscripts, consigning the key to his friend Fräulein Nevar; she arranged for a car to take him to the station, and placed in it a bunch of red roses. Various Munich acquaintances were there to see him off, Clara too, and Lou Andreas-Salomé. The latter had been

Rilke's guest for most of April and May: 'If I look back at Munich I see only Rainer'. She thought that private conversation between them was 'hardly necessary any longer: we felt almost at one in the solemn simplicities: Rilke could be like a boy and as he was nearly a quarter of a century ago'. Elizabeth Schmidt-Pauli was supposed to come to a station further down the line to say farewell before he crossed the border.

On his departure the flat was sub-let. Rosa kept expecting him to return, which Rilke from time to time intended to do, and she forwarded his mail at very irregular intervals. There were rumours among his friends that he was on the point of coming back, especially at the end of 1919, but he was put off by reports that foreigners were being sent out of Bavaria and that his flat would certainly be taken over. Elizabeth Schmidt-Pauli phoned the flat one day only to be told that Rilke had gone. They had arranged long ago that Rilke would call her before his departure, but Rosa informed the astonished Elizabeth that Rilke thought she would 'know' she had to meet him. She blamed herself for having failed the poet.

XIV

The Waiting Room

Lou Andreas-Salomé, who left Munich a few minutes before Rilke, recorded that even while they talked and joked as the train slowly moved off, she was overcome by a strange presentiment, remembering a melancholy phrase from Rilke's old Paris letters: 'I go as the animals go, when the beauty is past...'. It was the last time she saw him, though they continued to write. For Clara too it was a momentous leave-taking: she did not see her husband again for five years.

A new world had grown up, a world of passports, regulations and rations, utterly unlike the continent where he had travelled freely before the war. In the Swiss train Rilke was so nervous that the lady opposite spoke to him. He told her that he was not at all sure he would not be turned back at the frontier at the last moment.

'You follow me, and do what I do. They know me well because I often do this trip. If they think you are a friend of mine everything will be all right, you'll see.'

He did not tell her his name. When they began to talk about books, she proved to have very decided views about literature.

'Do you like poetry?' he ventured to ask.

'Oh yes, Goethe, and Heine, but amongst the moderns the only one I have any liking for is Rainer Maria Rilke.'

'How lovely,' he murmured discreetly.

When they finally stood on the platform in Switzerland, he saw her being greeted by a male acquaintance:

'I didn't know you knew Rilke!'

'I don't!' he heard her say.

'But you've just been talking to him!' She turned and stared, they all laughed, and Rilke came forward with his card and a promise to keep in touch.

After Zurich, his first stop was Nyon, on the lake of Geneva, where he stayed with Countess Mary Dobržensky. Rilke found the chalet unsuitable, and although he stayed there for a fortnight at the beginning of October, he complained of the number of guests crowded into the house: 'it looks like a salt cellar, and my little corner in it is like Saint Alexis' under the stairs, only that I can't exercise his radiant anonymity' (letter to Frau Nölke, 5 October 1919). In June he moved from Geneva to Berne, in July went on to Zurich, to Sils-Baselgia where he spent a few relaxed days with the Danish translators of *Malte,* thence to Soglio.

There he found his first breathing-space, staying in the Palazzo Salis, whose owner had befriended him. For nearly a month he took no thought of the future, revelling in a house full of old family possessions, the garden with traditionally clipped box hedges and a riot of summer flowers, the chestnut woods dipping towards Italy, and 'the crowning seduction of all', the ancient Salis library, normally inaccessible to guests but opened for Rilke's use. With a kind of foreknowledge he was looking for the room in which the *Elegies* were to be completed, always hovering in his mind like a promise and a duty. Only when he reached Soglio did he feel that Switzerland was not entirely devoid of the order and security for which he was searching. As he wrote later to Kippenberg about Soglio: 'everything there was like an indication of the future, like trying on material which will provide one later with a whole suit, a cloak and hood of invisibility' (5 October).

It took some time, however, for Rilke to reconcile himself to Switzerland and the Swiss scenery. Writing to Gertrud Knoop on 12 September, he described the strain of travelling at last, and Switzerland's luxury product: nature.

> You no longer knew how to set about it; you ... spent half the day reading the names Houbigant, Roger & Gallet and Pinaud over the drug-stores; yes, for a moment *this* was freedom, — who would have thought it possible? ... A mountain? behold, dozens of them on either hand, one behind the other; a lake? but certainly, and a very refined lake of the best quality, with reflections in purest water, a whole gallery of reflections with God himself to act as guide, explaining each in turn, unless of course he happens to be busy in his capacity as stage-manager, directing the spotlight of sunset on to the mountains. ... I cannot help it, the only way I can approach this assortment of nature is by being ironical. I remember the happy days when I used to draw the curtains in my compartment as I passed through Switzerland. ... It is odd too that psychoanalysis (at

least in Zurich) has assumed its most persuasive form here: nearly all these clean and angular young people are being analysed. Imagine the result: a sterilized Swiss, whose every corner has been swept out and scrubbed. What kind of inner life can find a place in this mind, which is as disinfected as an operating theatre, and as garishly illuminated?

Rilke left Soglio on 21 September for Begnins-sur-Gland, where he had arranged to meet Marthe. They spent a week together, and at its close Rilke wrote about their reunion in resigned, gentle terms to Frau Nölke:

> ... [through her] I hoped to knit myself gently back on to the violent fracture of the fatal year '14. How far I've succeeded I can't yet say — I recognize her, and recognize myself in her lively and undistorted remembrance — and yet we are no longer the same.... In any case it is a great thing to have invoked the past so directly — it responds — and merely to hear such a response resounding in my present *Lebensraum* makes it seem more familiar to me.   (29 September 1919)

There was then the lecture tour to be planned and executed: two lectures in Zurich first, where Rilke made the acquaintance of one of his greatest friends, Frau Nanny Wunderly-Volkart; St Gallen, Lucerne, Berne; Basle, where he was introduced to Frau Helene Burckhardt-Schatzmann and to the von der Mühll-Burckhardts, who offered him hospitality; finally to Winterthur, where he met the Reinhart brothers. Each lecture was cleverly adapted to its milieu. The first part invariably consisted of reading from his own work in fluent French or Italian, the second was introduced by a chat on some subject of local interest; in Winterthur, for example, on the local collection of Cézannes. Rilke warned Kippenberg that he could expect no money from the tour, as the clubs were poor and the dates too far apart, so that he had used up the fee for one lecture by the time the next came along. Though Kippenberg sent him as much as possible, the German marks melted away in Switzerland, and in Germany inflation was beginning.

The search for a place to live continued. 'On the invitation of a friend which I (there is no other word for it) "provoked"', Rilke set out to inhabit the garden-house in a property near Ascona, but it was uninhabitable, so he went to the Pension Villa Muralto in Locarno where he spent a disgruntled three months. At the end of February

1920, the Burckhardt sisters offered him the use of Schönenberg, near Pratteln; Rilke occupied it from March to June, except for a week's stay with Frau Wunderly-Volkart, and used it as his headquarters all summer, yet spoke of it as 'a kindly offered but inhospitable house'. At one point he was actually considering returning to Germany, but was advised against it on a chance meeting with Prince Alexander von Hohenlohe.

Instead he turned to Princess Marie, asking her to meet him in Venice. They had about a week together before she went on, and Rilke moved into the familiar mezzanino in the Palazzo Valmarana, where he had received the Duse in 1913. Being able to pick up the threads of his pre-war existence proved an unnerving experience, which finds expression in a letter to Frau Nölke (24 June 1920):

> For this is really the first time I have been 'outside'.
> Switzerland is merely a waiting-room to me, all the more
> because I found no memories to renew there.... Finding
> everything unaltered here answers the wish I brought with me
> in secret, but I didn't think of the other side of this hope, the
> painful one, that I'm unaltered too!... Fundamentally I have a
> great fear of mere repetition (except for moments in which
> repetition creates rhythm), and here a great deal is demanded
> of me once again, in a repetition the like of which I cannot
> ever remember, because at other times either the object or
> oneself had changed, or at any rate the dividing air between
> had become different, or the light, or the sensitivity of the eye.
> Now I'm being punished for having forced myself to lead a
> subdued existence all the time of the disasters...

When the replay of his past was about to include the arrival of the Duse, Rilke fled Venice. He wrote to Nanny Wunderly-Volkart that he intended to look for a place where he could expose himself to 'the dangers' of his work, that Soglio was a possibility but that he feared that any return to Switzerland would be brief, for financial reasons. He talked and wrote in a similar strain the whole summer and autumn, nevertheless managing a peripatetic Swiss existence between hotels and great family houses. No one would offer him a piece of the future, 'un bloc d'avenir' as he put it. Katherine Kippenberg procured for him an invitation from Prince Egon Fürstenberg to a house in the park of a German castle; the Valmaranas offered a place near Padua; Princess Marie renewed her offer of Lautschin in Bohemia. All these Rilke declined, having discovered Castle Berg on the Irchel, and the pleasures of Geneva, 'never so beautiful, so spacious, so airy, fluttering, almost floating, and recalling so much of what I vaguely comprehend under the name of Paris' (to Frau Nölke, 18 August).

Geneva offered two particular attractions: the Russian producer Georges Pitoëff and the painter Madame Baladine Klossowska ('Merline'). Pitoëff had established a new kind of puppet theatre; his genius so impressed Rilke that he even entertained the idea of becoming Pitoëff's secretary. The idea of Rilke at this stage touring Europe with a theatre company is almost as incongruous as the vision of him traversing the desert as part of an archaeological expedition. His admiration for Pitoëff's theatre, however, was quite genuine and he went so far as to say that masks and mime were the only valid alternatives for the contemporary stage, from which drama itself had disappeared. Although he offered the director's work as the reason for prolonging his stay in Geneva, Merline's presence was just as compelling, if not more so. Rilke had met her and her art-historian husband years ago in Paris, through Ellen Key; meeting again in Paris some years later, she informed him that she now had 'two charming sons'. Their intimate friendship only began to develop in August 1920, in Geneva and in time snatched as the two shuttled between cities. At the end of the month Rilke was in Berne; near the city he glimpsed a chestnut alley, iron gates, and behind them a steep little castle.

> An avenue like this, and a house like this, for the space of a year, and I would be saved. I felt that if only I could walk straight up to that house and into a quiet study awaiting me, I should start to work this very evening....

He wrote to Frau Wunderly of this sight of Castle Hollinger (22 August):

> I went close up to the park gate... and an evening bird was whistling in the park trees, one solitary bird; whistling as if it were asking if the silence was deep enough to feel its tone. It was.

She did her best to find such a place for Rilke, getting Colonel Ziegler to offer him the sole use of Castle Berg, with the services of a perfect housekeeper, Leni. With that prospect secure, Rilke made a dash for Paris.

He stayed at the Hotel Foyot, rue de Tournon, 22–29 October, and wrote to the Countess M. ecstatically on the 27th:

> What can I say, everything is good, completely and absolutely good; for the first time since those terrible years I am feeling the continuity of my life, which I was on the point of renouncing: for even Switzerland only perpetuated... the breaks, but here, here — *la même plénitude de vie, la même intensité, la même justice dans le mal*...
>
> I fit on to all the breaks and now I no longer feel them. If I could stay here I would have my life back again tomorrow, all its dangers, all its raptures: my whole life — *ma vie, depuis toujours mienne* — But the exchange prohibits this... now I *know* again, my mind has thrown off its fetters, I have ceased being rooted to one spot, I circle once more in my consciousness.

In the notebook he bought to keep a journal of the Paris visit, Rilke wrote only one sentence: *'Ici commence l'indicible'*. He had been aware of all that he risked in going to France, 'a sense of loss, a separation, an aversion', but as he explained to Hans Reinhart, 'I am in the fortunate position of appealing to *things* always; these and the air that danced and sparkled across from them had the same undiminished power over me...' (19 November).

On 12 November he moved into Schloss Berg am Irchel, whence he wrote contentedly to Frau Nölke:

> ... when I came back from Paris, with my need for quiet and reflection grown almost excessive, the place was there, ready for it, and arranged exactly so as to afford me all that.
>
> Really, *all that:* Berg is a quiet, strongly built, habitable house, full of strengthening forces, the after-effects of some entirely good and active past; the park, in front of the quiet windows, melts into the fields, which mount gently towards the Irchel, and the latter, a wooded, soft-contoured hill, shuts in the view without cramping it in the least. In the unbordered pool in front of the house a slender fountain rises day and night, and hardly a sound is to be heard above its own. No railway, no neighbours, and as if to make the shelter still more secure, all roads stopped on account of foot-and-mouth disease!

At the same time, he was aware that the congenial circumstances left him with no excuses as to his work, as he stated plainly to the Countess M. (25 November): 'My meeting with Paris — which was so healing

— puts me under an obligation, and now this obligation looms up all round me, clear and categorical, — if I fail this time, in Schloss Berg, I am past help.'

Rilke's preoccupation with the past of such old houses and their families indicates a need almost to make peace with the dead before he could carry on with his work. There was no clue here as to what had gone before. As he was settling down by the fireplace in the drawing-room one evening, he reported to the Kippenbergs and Princess Marie, he saw a gentleman dressed in eighteenth-century clothes sitting on the other side, who for three nights dictated verses to him. To Frau Wunderly, he gave a more sceptical account of the poems' composition (30 November):

> I wanted to find the trace of some previous occupant of Berg. A book in the library perhaps: but one evening see, see, who was that? I imagined superficially a figure. The circumstances came to my assistance but the book in question did not appear, in spite of my imagination. What was one to do but make one? And here it is: Poems. On the first page you will read: from the papers of Count C.W. Curious things for which I take no responsibility.... Seriously, I did not know what it was all about. It was fascinating and made me go on.

Incapable of working himself, Rilke had to invent someone who would do it for him. They were poems made with the same kind of concentration women give to knitting, he said. He refused to acknowledge them, or to include them in his published works.

He tried to preserve the solitary conditions necessary to his work, dissuading Ruth from paying him a visit that winter. Rilke consulted Kippenberg over her requests for her nineteenth birthday: clothes for the winter, music, art, French and maths lessons, a little pocket-money; he asked his publisher to see to all of them, and to give her the sum she would have spent on travelling to Switzerland. At the same time he was receiving reports from Merline of bad health, which so worried him that on a slim pretext of business he left Berg for Berne, and arrived in Geneva unexpectedly on 6 January 1921. Rilke took Merline to Berg for a week at the end of the month, and she visited him again for one day in February, when he read her a poem he had just discovered in the *Nouvelle revue française* Valéry's 'Cimetière Marin'. The emotional ups and downs of these months, and the interruptions,

were not conducive to work, but Rilke obliquely defended them in a
letter to the Countess M. (10 March):

> But even for me asceticism is out of the question. Since in the
> last analysis my creative powers proceed from the plainest
> adoration of life, from the daily inexhaustible wonder at it
> (how could I have been productive otherwise?) I would see it
> as a lie to reject any one of the currents that flow towards me.
> Any such denial would revenge itself by appearing as hardness
> in my art, however much the latter might gain potentially by
> such a denial: for who can be open and affirmative on such
> sensitive ground if he has a mistrustful, restrictive and timid
> attitude towards life!

In mid-March he began to translate Valéry's poems, which proved a
fruitful exercise, yet he could not produce the kind of work he had
hoped for by the time he left Berg for good, on 10 May.

Rilke went to a pension, Le Prieuré, at Etoy in the Vaud. He had
abandoned all hope of completing the elegies, of which the first four
were finished; there were fragments of the sixth, written in Ronda and
Paris in 1913, fragments of the ninth composed at Duino in March
1912, and parts of the tenth begun at Duino in 1912, completed in Paris
in 1913 but later rejected in that form. He had once written to Dory
von der Mühll about the absolute solitude and peace Duino — which
was destroyed in the war — had provided, and how he longed to take
up the work commenced there: 'But in order to do this I need the same
kind of uninterruptedness and inwardness which a mineral has in the
interior of a mountain when it is turning into a crystal' (24 December
1919). In the absence of such solitude, he decided to publish the
sequence as it stood. Princess Marie came to the Vaud for a week in
June to see her grandchildren, and Rilke read her the poems, telling her
of his intention. She was horrified, and worked hard to dissuade him
from publication, convinced that he would be able to finish them
properly. Again the Princess offered him asylum at Lautschin; there
was a possibility of going to Carinthia in the Black Forest; the
Countess Schaumburg offered her castle in Bohemia, while Elizabeth
Schmidt-Pauli undertook to investigate seven German castles for
Rilke: all in an effort to replace Schloss Berg. Meanwhile Rilke and
Merline set out for Sierre in the Valais, a region they had visited
together the previous October. They could not find a suitable house
for the winter and were on the eve of departure, when they saw in a

hairdresser's window an advertisement for a little château, a thirteenth century manor-house for sale or rent. This was the Château de Muzot, about twenty minutes above Sierre: a severe little tower with two floors and rooms furnished partly in seventeenth-century style, but without water or electricity. The rent seemed too dear and the place uninhabitable in many ways, yet Rilke was powerfully drawn by it and in his first letter on the subject to Frau Wunderly said, 'this is my château in Switzerland, perhaps'. The landscape he loved already because it blended those of Spain and Provence; he was happy to discover from a book on Valais that certain flowers and butterflies were common to all three places. Frau Wunderly again took matters in hand. She approached Werner Reinhart, who agreed to rent the house and put it at Rilke's disposal; later he bought it outright for Rilke to use for the rest of his life. Having made the decision to move there, at least for the winter, Rilke was still very uncertain about committing himself, while Merline simply got on with the business of making Muzot attractive and comfortable. Frau Wunderly inundated the house with practical gifts, from soap to sofa, yet the process remained tentative with neither Rilke nor Muzot yielding to the other.

Rilke found out what he could of Muzot's history, and reported to Princess Marie the story of Isabelle de Chevron, whose husband Jean de Montheys had been killed at the battle of Marignan shortly after their marriage. Thereupon two suitors fought a duel over the girl and killed each other. Isabelle lost her mind and took to wandering to their graves at night, 'très légèrement habillée', where she was eventually found dead. 'So somehow we shall have to resign ourselves to the ghosts of Isabelle and Jean de Montheys returning like pendulums from Marignan, and not be surprised at anything.' (25 July 1921)

Minor worries persisted but a major one was allayed when a young woman was engaged as housekeeper. Frieda Baumgarten served a brief apprenticeship in Frau Wunderly's house, and was carefully instructed by Merline when she came to Muzot. She remained in Rilke's service until his death. Merline left on 8 November; when Rilke wrote gratefully to her, he mentioned that she had forgotten to take away her postcard of 'Orpheus', which she had pinned up on the wall facing his desk and never reclaimed. He was delighted to find that the boy who delivered his milk was called 'Essaye': on such tiny omens his inspiration and decision to stay were nourished. 'Ce muzotisme qui a failli devenir une espèce de maladie sera au bout de compte quand même une croyance — espérons-le!'

Rilke's whereabouts became more widely circulated than he had wished, through the announcement of his daughter's engagement. He would not promise to attend to the wedding ceremony, left the financial arrangements to Anton Kippenberg, and apart from some benevolent letters to Ruth and her fiancé, Carl Sieber, guarded his solitude from this potential incursion. In reply to a letter from an old family friend, Gertrud Knoop, he spoke of being generally confident over Ruth's choice: 'I think Ruth will become a squire's wife, and this steady and active life would suit her inclinations and capabilities very well...' (26 November). This reopening of their correspondence proved to be of great importance. At the time he was writing an enormous number of letters, few of them less than four pages long: he described his correspondents to Ruth as young women and girls, terribly lonely even in the midst of their families; young married women, furious at what had befallen them; young workers, mostly revolutionary, coming blindly out of state prisons, taking refuge in literature and writing angry poems.

The least thing might still have influenced him to leave Muzot altogether. Privately he thought himself slightly crazy to have come at all, yet there was no lack of design in his choosing Muzot. Rilke used to say 'J'aime quand le cercle se renferme'. If he had not been able to repeat his Duino experience at will, it was partly because there was something in him reluctant to repeat such terrifying work, and his subsequent choice of residences betrayed that. None of them had the austerity of Duino, the remoteness and cloistral air of devotion, until he saw Muzot. Nevertheless he had used Duino as a hard casing for his sensitive spirit, as a shelter and not a moral discipline. Rilke compared living at Muzot to putting on armour. Paul Valéry in his memoir of Rilke (in *Les Cahiers du Mois* 23/24, 1926) saw it as a place where memory and solitude could reach an absolute pitch, where the only thing to be heard was 'le monologue infini d'une conscience tout isolée, que rien ne distrait de soi-même et du sentiment d'être unique'. Here Rilke's eyes were to be fixed on man's ascent, not on the Fall except in the last words of the elegies, where 'falling' is seen as the greatest wonder of all.

XV

The Unending Monologue

In Muzot, Rilke was trying to transport himself back over ten years to the period before the war when the elegies grew in Duino and Toledo. He had not been waiting for inspiration so much as trying to recover some of the freshness he had once possessed. The 'poetry' he had been expecting in fact consisted in an abandonment of poetry, much as the philosophy of Wittgenstein consisted in the abandonment of philosophy. He was brought face to face with 'reality' as he had not been since writing *Malte*.

On New Year's Day 1922 Rilke received from Gertrud Knoop the letter he had requested, describing the death of her daughter Vera. This girl had been a playmate of Ruth's and had died two years earlier, just emerging from adolescence. She had been beautiful, artistically gifted and a wonderful dancer. Rilke closed his reply to Frau Knoop: 'But for me it has come as an immense obligation to my innermost and gravest self... that I am allowed, on the first evening of a New Year, to take into my possession *these* pages.' The account meant more to him than anything had done for a long time — as a symbol.

The striking thing about Rilke's series of requiems had been his skill in using others as symbols of his own inner states. He had used Paula's death in that way, and the 'Requiem on the Death of a Boy' (November 1915) was largely filled with images of his own childhood: 'Sometimes close to the house I sat and watched a bird. / If I could have become that watching!' 'I loved no one. / Loving, you see, was fear ...' ('Zuweilen, dicht am Hause, sass ich lange / und schaute einem Vogel nach.' 'Keinen hatt ich lieb. / Liebhaben war doch Angst —, begreifst du ...') Amidst fluctuating human emotions, Rilke made the boy aware of the solidity of things:

> You talked, you laughed, but none of you
> was in the talking and the laughter. No.
> Nothing changed as you all changed,

neither the sugar-bowl, nor the glass of wine.
The apple lay. How good it often was
to grasp the firm round apple...

Ihr spracht, ihr lachtet, dennoch war ein jeder
im Sprechen nicht und nicht im Lachen. Nein.
So wie ihr alle schwanktet, schwankte weder
die Zuckerdose, noch das Glas voll Wein.
Der Apfel lag. Wie gut das manchmal war,
den festen vollen Apfel anzufassen...

What he had grasped about himself was his inability to 'love' in the pure sense he had once believed possible; he had become aware of the dominating 'sensualité de l'âme', in his own words.

One of Rilke's difficulties was to know exactly how to approach his subject. He had learned from Rodin how to control inspiration, and he expected his conscious mind to take over. Instead, on 2 February, he felt himself so moved that he began to write not the elegies he had wanted but a series of sonnets, addressed to Orpheus and dedicated to Vera.

Within three days he had written twenty-six sonnets, copies of which he sent to Professor Strohl in Zurich and to Frau Knoop. On 9 February Rilke despatched another sonnet 'as it came to me this morning on waking' to Frau Knoop to replace the twenty-first, which seemed to him 'empty'. The same evening he cabled Frau Wunderly: 'Seven elegies now practically complete. Joy and wonder.'

It was, in Rilke's words, a question of 'monstrous obedience'; he could do nothing but write frantically. The sonnets were utterly unexpected, and yet formed a real counterpart to the freer and more dangerous elegies. This kind of dualism had occurred previously: *The Book of Hours* paralleled by the *Tales of God, New Poems* by *Malte*. When writing to the Polish translator of the *Elegies*, Rilke pointed out that the *Sonnets to Orpheus* were of the same 'birth':

... the fact that they arose suddenly in connection with the premature death of a young girl brings them still nearer to their original fountain-head; for this connection is another point of contact with the centre of that kingdom whose depth and influence we share, boundlessly, with the dead and the unborn.... In that most vast, *open* world all beings are — one cannot say 'contemporaneous', for it is precisely the passage of Time which determines that they all *are*. This transitoriness rushes everywhere into a profound Being.   (13 November 1925)

On the way home from sending his telegram, Rilke discovered how to flesh out the skeletons of the eighth and ninth elegies. By 11 February he had completed the tenth, and at once wrote to Kippenberg, Lou and the Princess, and to Merline in Berlin: 'Je suis sauvé!'

> All in a few days, it was an unspeakable storm, a tornado of the spirit (as in Duino), the very fibres and tissues cracked in me — there was never a thought of eating, God knows what nourished me.
>   But now it is done. Done.
>   Amen.
>   So here is the triumph I was holding out for, through everything. Through everything. This was what I wanted. Just this and nothing more.
>   One I have dedicated to Kassner. The whole thing is yours, Princess, how should it not be! It'll be called:
>   'The Duino Elegies'.
>   In the book (for I cannot give you what has belonged to you from the beginning) there will be no dedication, only:
>   'The property of Marie...'

Rilke wrote with the same exultation to Lou:

> And imagine, there's *something else,* in another connection, beforehand (in *Sonnets to Orpheus* — twenty-five sonnets written suddenly, as a preliminary to the storm, in memory of Vera Ouckama Knoop) I wrote, or rather *created* the horse, you remember, the prancing happy white horse with the peg at his foot, which suddenly sprang towards us one evening in a meadow by the Volga:
>   HOW
> oh how I made him, an 'ex-voto' for Orpheus! — What is time? When is the present? Across many years he leapt towards me, whole in his happiness, into my open heart.
>   So they came, one after another.
>   Now I *know* myself again. It was like a crippling of my being that the elegies were not there.

> They are. They are!
> I have gone out and stroked my little Muzot for having
> guarded all this for me and at last granted it to me, stroked it
> like a great shaggy beast.

Even then he was not to rest, for between the twelfth and twentieth of the month he produced another elegy to replace the fifth: 'thus I even have the *Saltimbanques* who affected me so when I was first in Paris and have lain on me like a task ever since,' he reported to Lou on the twentieth, adding that the sonnets had also continued; he had composed twenty-nine more. The last poem from this great storm began, 'Meaningful word, "inclination"!' ('Neigung: wahrhaftes Wort!') and closed joyfully: 'How could we ever be cheated, / ever betrayed, we with every reward / over-rewarded...' ('Wie könnten wir jemals Verkürzte / oder Betrogene sein: wir mit jeglichem Lohn / längst Überlohnten...'). When he sent the lines to the Kippenbergs in December 1923, it was with the wish 'that this attitude (achieved here, at Muzot) which they express may remain ever more validly and enduringly mine'.

Lou warned him to beware of his reaction to the terrific strain he had been under, but for once she was apparently wrong. Rilke remained quietly in Muzot, visited by the Kippenbergs and Princess Marie in the spring; Merline spent August with him and then they both went to Beatenberg near Lake Thun. His letters that autumn were full of anxiety over the prospects for Merline and her sons; he had promises of help from Gide and Frau Nölke but when the doubling of German railway fares was announced, Merline and her younger son rushed to cross the frontier, heading for Berlin. 'I have hardly ever had such a ghastly feeling that I was letting someone I loved fall into the abyss,' Rilke wrote to Frau Nölke on 1 December, adding that he found it 'painful to see these delightful, intensely gifted children living at the caprice of fortune, alternately on the emptiness and over-fullness of unorganized life'.

He described his own regular and solitary life to Merline (19 December 1922): the morning given over to correspondence, the afternoon to translating Valéry's poems, the evening spent reading; late to bed and late to rise. In this impersonal world he was content; in reply to a letter from Ilse Jahr (2 December) he admitted 'my world begins with *things*, — and thus even the least person in it is frighteningly large, almost an exaggeration'.

But already I am directing you further afield, beyond me, to
the figure whom I build more truly and more lastingly, outside.
Cling to *it* if it appears great and significant to you. Who
knows what I am? I change and change. But that figure is the
limit of my changing, its pure rim ...

In his New Year letter to Lou, Rilke said that he had never worked on
translations with such certainty and insight as he was bringing to
Valéry, and that he had everything he needed within Muzot, although
his health was 'going through strange convulsions'.

That summer, after three weeks of dental treatment in Zurich and
time with Merline at Muzot, Rilke was sufficiently run-down to resort
to a sanatorium cure at Schöneck bei Beckenried. From there he wrote
to Clara on 10 September, rather formally. She had not been among
those immediately notified of the completion of the elegies, but he
naturally sent her the finished volume:

You will understand the deep satisfaction, even happiness, it
gives me that you were able to accept the Elegies without
more ado, as a tuning-in and a harmony with those infinitely
consoling moments of insight which move you to the depths of
your nature, and put you far above the most concrete forms
of unhappiness.

He spent most of October at Meilen with Frau Wunderly, while
Merline supervised repairs and cleaning at Muzot where they both
lived in November. Rilke wrote that he had come to 'a couple of bad
chapters in his life', which nevertheless had to be read and com-
prehended like the others, 'only it was not so easy to understand'. He
saw it as a bad omen that the poplar tree near the house was felled
without warning, something that probably could have been prevented
had he protested in time: 'O Bäume Lebens, o wann winterlich?' ('O
trees of life, what are your signs of winter?').

Again he was forced to go to a sanatorium, this time to Valmont
near Montreux, on 29 December. It was a fearful illness: 'I had come to
another level of existence, perhaps to that where the incurables are.'
Rilke was reminded of the time when he was made to wear a uniform:
'Just as at that time, nine years ago, looking out from my bed, Nature,
even trees, were no longer present to my gaze. I could no longer reach
them. I was elsewhere. When I received your flowers,' he wrote to
Frau Wunderly, 'I knew what it was: I was separated from them, as if

by a pane of glass' (21 January 1924). The sickness, whose cause was
undiagnosed, bewildered him; he told Frau Knoop that he found all the
dealings with doctors 'terribly confusing':

> ... not unlike suddenly having to commune with my soul
> through the devious agency of a priest: for my association with
> my body has, for twenty-five years, been so straightforward
> and of so strict an understanding that I feel this medical
> interpreter sticking like a wedge into our joint agreement.... I
> was convinced that all the elements of my nature worked
> together towards a pure harmony with creation issuing at the
> apex, springing forth from this abundance of common (physical
> and spiritual) gladness.   (13 February)

Rilke interpreted his illness to Lou as the expected 'recoil' from the
previous winter's exertions, but wrote to her cheerfully on 22 April
when he was busy with a welcome succession of visitors:

> But I have not recanted, either, what I wrote to you two years
> ago: that after so magnificent a triumph I would gladly bear
> anything that might be laid on me by way of reaction. I am
> holding out. And have not been wholly inactive: a complete
> volume of French poems ... has unaccountably come into being,
> with much else besides, and my reading was lively all through
> the winter and most fruitful in its results. My old tower is so
> situated that French books in particular can reach me: one's
> astonishment over what is being produced there knows no end.
> First and foremost, Proust — he will certainly be a marvel for
> you as well. You know that I translated Paul Valéry the winter
> before last: this year he was one of my first visitors in
> Muzot ...

The Kippenbergs came, and Clara in May. It was five years since they
had seen each other; she stayed for ten days that passed happily. Rilke
was particularly in need of affection and support then, so it was a well-
timed visit. Clara went on to meet Nanny Wunderly-Volkart, who
greatly approved of her, and said so to Rilke's pleasure. Rilke himself
left Muzot in June to stay with Werner Reinhart, to travel with Frau
Wunderly in her car, to take the waters at Ragaz in company with
Princess Marie. While there he received a letter from Nora Purtscher-
Wydenbruck, the Princess's niece, concerning her experiences with
mediumistic writing. They had just been discussing séances the

Princess had attended; the whole subject was freshly brought to Rilke's mind and in his reply he reflected at length on the spirit world. He had once believed that spiritual phenomena were caused by external agencies, but now he was no longer so inclined. As extensive as the external world was, it could hardly bear comparison with the dimensions of man's inner life, which did not even need the space of the universe to be in itself infinite. Rilke outlined his theory that consciousness was like the apex of a pyramid, and that at the deeper, broader level simple Being could become an event, 'the inviolable presence and simultaneity of all that we, on the upper "normal" apex of consciousness, are only permitted to experience as flux'. He wanted to emphasise that séances revealed only one kind of mystery among many, things

> rather to be suffered than acknowledged; rather not repudiated
> than invoked; rather consented to and loved than questioned
> and made use of. I am, forunately, completely unserviceable as
> a medium, but I do not doubt for one moment that, in my own
> way, I keep myself open to the influence of those often
> homeless powers, and that I never cease to enjoy or sustain
> their companionship.... For the rest, it belongs to the original
> tendencies of my nature to accept the Mysterious *as such...*
> that is mysterious to its very depths and is so
> everywhere...   (11 August)

He returned to Muzot for August, was on the move again in September, including a visit to Lausanne where he met Edmond Jaloux, but returned to Valmont at the end of November for a costly and none too helpful stay of two months. In early January 1925 Rilke departed for Paris, in a last attempt to forget all about his illness. Paris had never failed him, and since the publication of *Malte* in French in 1923 he had been inundated by invitations. He remained in Paris for over seven months, living at the Hotel Foyot. Merline had moved to Paris in May, and Rilke visited her nearby house almost daily; he saw Valéry less than he had hoped, as the French poet was preoccupied with the arrangements for his election to the Academy, and Gide too, who was preparing to leave for Africa. He saw much of Edmond Jaloux, and made new acquaintances: Charles du Bos, Ivan Bunin, Princess Bibesco. For weeks Rilke spent the mornings going over the translation of *Malte* with Maurice Betz. Despite these intellectual and social pleasures, Rilke reported miserably to Lou:

But neither victory nor relief came to me. Imagine that the
obsession... was stronger and mightier than Paris. It became
the suffering of one long defeat; and if I greatly out-stayed my
time in Paris, right into August, this was only because I was
ashamed to return to my tower in the same fetters as before.

He left abruptly on 18 August, without even taking leave of his friends,
and Merline accompanied him on a restless tour of towns in Burgundy,
via Sierre to Lake Maggiore, Milan, Baveno and back to Sierre. She
stayed with him until he left for Ragaz, whence he continued to
Meilen and then Berne. His illness broke out as an infection of the
mouth that hindered his speech. Rilke was terrified that he might have
cancer.

Amidst this constant fear he composed his last will and testament at
Muzot on 27 October 1925, and sent it sealed to Frau Wunderly, by
now his closest friend. He stipulated that there should be no priest at
his bedside 'should anything happen': he avoided where he could all
mention of the word death. 'Should I fall into a severe illness which
might finally disorder my reason', he wrote, he wanted to have the
arrangements for his burial made clear. He did not wish to be buried in
the precincts of Muzot, where he might disturb the ghost of Isabelle de
Montheys, but at Raron, where he had so often stood 'to receive the
wind and light of this landscape'. His gravestone was to be simple and
flat, and he had composed his own epitaph.

For the great event of his fiftieth birthday young literary France
produced its homage in the form of *Reconnaissance pour Rilke*. In his
contribution, Maurice Betz said that at a time when French poetry
inclined to Mallarmean experiments in an exhausted form on the one
hand, and to become an object of experience, under surrealism, on the
other, it was moving to discover a poetic approach deeply human in
tone and sensibility. Readers, he said, were also seduced by the infinite
nuances of an art 'deriving, through its gentle plasticity, unerringly
from a Latin tradition'. In a November letter to Clara, Rilke marked
out his fiftieth year as the most fundamental crisis of his life: 'instead of
seeing clearly as *you* have learnt to do, I see black, and this casts
confusion and darkness over everything.' He worked on the cor-
rections of the definitive edition of his works, whose publication he
had authorized when Kippenberg visited him in 1924, but had to admit
he was really ill: 'I am like an empty place; I *am* not; I am not even
identical with my misery.'

Writing to various people over this period, including Edmond Jaloux, Rilke considered the matter of Christianity especially in relation to sex. He felt that a new religion was needed, allowing a proper place to natural instincts instead of thwarting and repressing them as Christianity had done: 'Why have they made our sex homeless?' Just as we conjure death out of our lives by facile optimism, so do we eliminate love from the senses; Rilke was fighting for the whole man.

> Physical experience is a sensory experience, like pure vision, or pure feeling, like the taste of a lovely fruit on the tongue. It is a great and infinite experience which is given to us, a knowledge of the world... And it is not wrong of us to accept it; it is wrong that almost all of us abuse and waste this experience, and that we use it as a stimulus when we are bored, instead of as a means for reaching the heights... If only he were more respectful towards his own fruitfulness, which is one and the same, whether spiritual or physical...

In the posthumously-published 'Letter from a Young Worker' (written in early February 1922), Rilke had asked:

> Why, if they are anxious to help us, helpless as we so often are, why leave us in the lurch at the very roots of all experience? Anyone supporting us *there* could rest assured that we would ask no more of him. For the assistance given there would grow by itself, as our life grew, and would become stronger and greater together with it. And never die away. Why do they not fit us into our closest being? Why do we have to creep about it, and finally, like burglars and thieves, get inside our own lovely sex, within which we wander around, butting into each other and slipping, only to hasten out at last, as if caught in the act, into the twilight of Christianity?... Why has our sex been made homeless for us, instead of being transformed into the fête of our maturity?

He wondered whether the sexes were not closer than was realised, and whether a renewal in the world might not come about through men and women seeking each other 'not as contraries, but as brother and sister and neighbour', finding a way 'to carry together in seriousness and patience the heavy burden of sex which has been laid upon them'. The notion of Christ as mediator necessary to a sinful world was repugnant to Rilke, a roundabout way of approaching the God who is never left behind. He wrote to Ilse Jahr (22 February 1923):

> The strong, inward, vibrant bridge of the Mediator has
> meaning only when the chasm between God and ourselves is
> admitted — but even this chasm is full of the darkness of God,
> and if anyone feels like it, let him go down into it and howl
> there (that is more necessary than crossing over it).

The disquieting aspect of the *Elegies* from this perspective was that they gave no evidence of any such descent into the abyss, although *Malte* was full of such howling. Instead there was the image of the mountain, an ascent towards the summit, and a mediator in the form of the Angel.

XVI

The Rose of Contradiction

Rilke was not released from Valmont until May, when he felt sufficiently well to stay in a nearby hotel, and later to meet Edmond Jaloux at Lausanne. Muzot was undergoing repairs so Rilke spent much of the summer in Ragaz, where Princess Marie and the Wunderly-Volkarts also stayed, and at the beginning of September went to stay with Frau Weininger in Lausanne. It may have been there that he made the acquaintance of the 'beautiful Egyptian', Madame Eloui Bey. He finally returned to Muzot in October and settled down to work. A Russian girl, Génia Tchernosvitow, was acting as his secretary; they read Russian together and Rilke dictated his Valéry translations to her. It was in that month that the peculiar accident occurred which precipitated his last illness.

The rose had become one of his favourite symbols. Rilke had mentioned it in the 'Requiem for a Friend' where it had indicated Paula's presence, he had associated roses with her since the Worpswede days when they decorated her Paris hat. And there was his dream of the maiden, in which he had felt an 'infinite desire to possess the life that had escaped him'; her lids had become roses. Even his friends were aware of the powerful associations the flower held for him. In the *Elegies* it had become the 'rose of pure seeing', and in his own epitaph it was the rose of pure contradiction. Taken together with his firm belief in dying his own death, there seems something fated about the fact that when gathering roses in the garden of Muzot, in preparation for a visit from Madame Eloui, he should have torn his finger on a thorn. She arrived two hours late to find Rilke waiting in the road; he said he had been following her journey from a distance and had known just when to expect her. The scratch did not seem important that day, but it soon set up an infection to which his condition made him prone. The other hand became inflamed. The symptoms enabled a diagnosis at last, but Rilke was by then far gone in leukaemia.

He returned to Valmont on 30 November 1926. At first he had visitors, whom he saw come and go like so many pictures. Years ago he had written about the Prodigal Son's return, how he had gone to the places he had loved most when a child:

> ... to the meadows perhaps, or under the tree in whose shade he had played. How small the hedges had become! And were these the ditches of which he had been so afraid? The hills in the distance had once been mountains. He looked around; he was quite alone. No one was following him any longer.

Soon he wanted to see only the doctor he trusted, a nurse who he insisted should be ignorant of his being a writer, and Frau Wunderly. The only letters he wanted were from Lou Andreas-Salomé, who he believed could help him. Messages from the doctor and sister went to her with Rilke's own, but her full replies conveyed neither consolation nor hope. A nurse reported that when she asked him whether to write to Lou again, 'he said no, with a wave of his hand'.

Frau Wunderly, recounting these days to Frau Nölke, recorded that Rilke said to her: 'Dear, help me to my death, I don't want the doctor's death — I want my freedom.' He was in great pain but steadily refused soporifics and drugs. Every morning the nurse read the 'Chronique mondaine' from *Le Figaro* to him, and in the afternoons Frau Wunderly read from the *Cahiers verts* for hours at a stretch; if she stopped, thinking him asleep, Rilke would call out 'Continuez!' He did not want to know the name of his illness, nor anything of its course. All over his body black blisters formed, which burst and bled; his mouth and nostrils were ulcerated, making drinking extremely difficult and painful though Rilke had a terrible thirst. He said that for two years he had had 'the feeling, the absolute certainty, that something was rising up in me to the infinite, and now the collapse has come'. His fear was that he would be disturbed in the possession of this fate, and he said to Dr Haemmerli who proposed to call in a consultant, 'Just think how awful it would be if a doctor came and destroyed all this with the banal consolations of a bedside manner'. Although Rilke's call to Frau Wunderly had been a note 'C'est l'enfer, jour et nuit!', he apparently managed to say to her once, 'Never forget, my dear, life is full of splendour'.

In conversations with Dr Haemmerli Rilke always stopped short of the word 'death'. He had always looked it straight in the face before, without any illusions yet with confidence in the unity of the here and

hereafter; he had created its dry image in 'Der Tod', written in
Munich in 1915.

> Da steht der Tod, ein bläulicher Absud
> in einer Tasse ohne Untersatz.
> Ein wunderlicher Platz für eine Tasse:
> steht auf dem Rucken einer Hand. Ganz gut
> erkennt man noch an dem glasierten Schwung
> den Bruch des Henkels. Staubig. Und: '*Hoff-nung*'
> an ihrem Bug in aufgebrauchter Schrift.
>
> Das hat der Trinker, den der Trank betrifft,
> bei einem fernen Frühstück ab-gelesen.
>
> Was sind denn das für Wesen,
> die man zuletzt wegschrecken muss mit Gift?
>
> Blieben sie sonst? Sind sie denn hier vernarrt
> in dieses Essen voller Hindernis?
> Man muss ihnen die harte Gegenwart
> ausnehmen wie ein künstliches Gebiss.
> Dann lallen sie. Gelall, Gelall . . . .
>
> O Sternenfall,
> von einer Brücke einmal eingesehn — :
> Dich nicht vergessen. Stehn!

> There stands death, a blue deposit
> in a cup without a saucer.
> A wonderful place for a cup:
> on the back of a hand. One sees
> quite well on the glazed curve
> the crack from the handle. Dusty. And 'Hope'
> inscribed upon its slope in faded writing.
>
> The drinker concerned with the drink read this
> at a breakfast long ago.
>
> What kind of creatures are they
> who must be frightened off at the end by poison?

Would they otherwise remain? Are they
infatuated with this food that is all obstacle?
The hard present has to be extracted
from them like a set of false teeth.
Then they gabble. Gabble, gabble....

O shower of falling stars,
perceived once from a bridge and forever,
never let me forget you! Stay!

At the words 'Gelall, Gelall' the form breaks because the irreducible
riddle of death advances into the forefront of consciousness, even there
only to be caught up again. The end of the poem, recalling a memory
of evening, is at the same time a cry of despair and its conquest through
beauty remembered.

Rilke had seen the acceptance of life and death as part of the same
thing, equally necessary. In writing to Witold von Hulewicz about the
Elegies (13 November 1925), he maintained:

To admit the one without the other would, it is here realized
with exultation, be a limitation which would ultimately
exclude everything infinite. Death is the side of life which is
turned away from us, and upon which we shed no light. We
must try to widen our consciousness of existence so that it is at
home in both spheres, with no dividing-line between them, so
that we may draw endless sustenance from both. The true way
of life leads through both kingdoms, the great circulation of the
blood passes through both: there is neither a here nor a
hereafter but a single great unity in which the beings who
transcend us, the angels, have their habitation.

It is thought that Rilke knew he was going to die only three days
before he did so. 'Don't tell me how things are going,' he said to Dr
Haemmeli. 'Please. When you come in, don't speak to me if I am
asleep, but press my hand so that I know you are there. And I shall press
your hand, like that. Then you will know I am awake. If I do not press
your hand, promise you will sit me upright and do something to bring
me back to the frontier of consciousness.' 'Meine Grenze' — the
frontier of consciousness, the border. Death had always been the
frontier for him, the touchstone, the gate. On the last night of all he
was conscious for a long time, but collapsed under an onslaught of

pain. An hour before his death on 29 December, he pressed the doctor's hand. In his account of Rilke's Swiss years, J.R. von Salis reports:

> Suddenly he looked up with wide-open blue eyes, like a healthy man, gazed for a long time in front of him, as though he were seeing someone, and convulsively pressed the hands that held him. It was impossible, in this visionary position, to tell that he was dead.

The funeral took place on Sunday, 2 January 1927. Four bearers carried the coffin up the steep icy path of the hill. In front, one man carried a wooden cross. During the mass inside the little church, organ and violin played the music of Johann Sebastian Bach. There were few mourners. The service over outside, the coffin was lowered into the grave, wreaths were laid upon it, and a great lamentation of bells broke over the valley of Raron. The epitaph on the simple stone was Rilke's own composition:

> Rose, oh reiner Widerspruch, Lust,
> Niemandes Schlaf zu sein unter soviel
> Lidern.

> Rose, o pure contradiction, joy,
> To be no one's sleep, under so many
> Lids.

The rose, which throughout his life had been the symbol of his love, and which in his Muzot garden had been possibly the immediate cause of his mortal illness, thus became on his tombstone his symbol of eternal life.

XVII

Affirmations

Rilke's fullest explanation of his own work is to be found in the letter to Hulewicz, his Polish translator, sent before he entered Valmont for the last time. It throws considerable light on whatever he possessed of a metaphysical system, although it is difficult to decide how much of the letter is explication and how much an elaboration of new ideas and new poems.

In *The Book of Hours,* God had been imaged as a cathedral, to be worked at; a justly medieval image. The only thing complete and great in the miserable lives of people then was the cathedral, towering above their preoccupations like a live thing. Today a spire is visible at best above the sea of roofs, like the mast of some wrecked ship. In that early collection, beliefs were less important in the last resort than scenes and figures, who cast their beliefs like shadows before them. The decisive factor was not so much the personal isolation of the poet as the breaking of his organic link with society. He felt an outcast. *The Book of Hours* is full of the spirit of the Middle Ages, when religion, adventure and love could be given adequate expression in the monastery, in some craft, in the career of arms, or in the life of knight, squire or troubadour; when social forms were in the process of construction. The characters who emerged, and in whom Rilke believed, were characters who renounced the world: beggars, monks, unhappy lovers, heroes who died young. Apart from the hierarchy of society, the world was chaotic. These are concepts that recur throughout Rilke's work, yet they are insufficient to form a philosophy. They are the images, in a sense, of his renunciation.

In *New Poems* he took a step forward, but only an apparent one: the world was no more ordered than it had ever been. The pressure of cities reduced Rilke to his childhood vision, when he felt he knew the world of things better than the world of people. He pursued the idea of the 'thing-in-itself', isolating individual things, trying to replace the loss of the organic link between himself and the world that love could have provided. No coherent world emerged from these efforts, and no philosophy, in spite of what Rodin had to teach him.

Instead his own feelings were seen as outlaws: courage, a lion; ruthlessness, a panther; beauty, flamingoes; grace, gazelles. Everything emphasized his exile, or as he himself put it, 'became rich and gave him up'. Finally he took refuge in people, but always of the same type: decadent Tsars, who had forgotten that it was not possible to rule merely through the symbols of rule, and whose real link with the people had gone; fair women, left to their own resources, to die or retire into nunneries; holy men of all kinds, mystics and saints; a hagiography of individuals with one thing in common, no more attachment to earth. Any tragic love could break such attachment.

The fear of death was a new theme in Rilke's work. It connects with those late medieval dances of death of which Holbein's woodcuts are a supreme expression. Each in the dance expects his *own* death, which for some will be merciful and mild, but for others hard and terrible; a new form of heroism gains ground among men, to look death bravely in the face despite the knowledge that in death one is alone. In a sense *Malte* is the result of a growing awareness of this process, and an expression of the terror it aroused in Rilke. He felt his identity with everything that was suffering. All the cripples and outcasts were his own outcast feelings, growing towards death. How they had come to this condition Rilke did not know, except that in some way they had lost the sense of the Divine, and their organic link with society. What was that natural link? How was it to be discovered and regained?

He had searched for the answer to those questions for the rest of his life. His growing concern with the fate of women in love, and with those he himself had loved, may have derived from an awareness that he had lost the link with society when a child. Again when he failed the women he loved, he may have realized that it was because of some quality in himself deriving from his upbringing, self-consciousness, perhaps terror, certainly something which froze his ability to love. Yet if life had become impossible, as Malte saw it, flight was still possible; even if one could not evade 'fate'.

In the Elegies, on the same given conditions, life becomes possible again, receives indeed the final affirmation which young Malte, although on the right track *'des longues études'*, could not make. *The affirmation of life and of death is seen to be one and the same thing in the Elegies. . . .*

... We, who exist in a transitory present, are not for a
single instant satisfied in the world of time, nor are we bound
to it; we are always taking leave and going over to those who
have lived previously, to the place of our origin, and to those
who apparently come after us. In that *open* and largest of
worlds, everything is — one cannot say contemporaneous for
the lapse of time itself means that they all *are*. All that passes
away, falls everywhere into deep Being.

Man's task, Rilke continued to Hulewicz, was to transform the world
of things and the world of phenomena into understanding, for:

We are the bees of the Invisible. 'Nous butinons éperdument le miel du
visible, pour accumuler dans la grande ruche d'or de l'Invisible.'
[We are continually madly plundering the honey of the visible,
in order to store it up in the great, golden hive of the
invisible.]

He then became more personal. The things about him were
disappearing, 'the lived and living things', and he thought his
generation were perhaps the last to know such things. Therefore their
human and 'laric', that is ancestral, worth had to be preserved, against
the terrible abstract world of the machine producing on a mass scale
things of no worth.

Rilke had often meditated on this problem of the machine-age.
Although in *The Book of Hours* he was inclined to reject the false reality
of the metropolis and its civilization, he later became more aware of
the inevitability of human development and understood that the
machines involved man in a gigantic struggle, whose outcome was not
yet decided. Merely to complain of such a world was pointless. It was
rather a question of how to withstand the claim of the machine to rule,
how to resist mankind's desire for organization and mechanistic
attitudes.

A purely human and living purpose should conquer youthful pride in
advancing machinery. In the *Sonnets to Orpheus* Rilke confronted the
present with the reality of the ancient world. All were involved in this
struggle for the future and each man's decision would be momentous
for final victory, which those now alive might not see. For Rilke it was
a question of proceeding from one form of reality to another, of
leaving a decadent age behind in order to go forward to a new age
which might resemble that ancient world bequeathed by the Greeks.

The earth had no choice, Rilke wrote, but to become in his sense 'invisible', that is, spiritual.

The Angels thus came nearer. 'The angel of the Elegies,' he told Hulewicz, 'is the Being who sees in the Invisible a higher order of reality: terrible, therefore for us, because we, who love and are transformed in him, still cling to the Visible.' Rilke had first seen the angels on the Christmas tree at home; they had sung hymns and that praise 'gave me the angels, the consciousness of whom, far from being lost, accompanied me at all stages of my life'. An entry in his diary dated 12 July 1912, when he was at San Vio, runs: 'Ach, da wir Hilfe von Menschen erharrten, stiegen Engel, lautlos, mit einem Schritte hinüber, über das liegende Herz.' ('When we were expecting aid from men, angels stepped silently across, over the surrendered heart.') The vision had always been with him.

Many passages in the *Elegies* are reminiscent of the poem for Paula, 'Requiem for a Friend'. Rilke had fought hard to acquire and conquer the consciousness of his inability to love. Love, as in the poem 'Turning', had seemed to him the most desirable quality in the universe, giving all the others meaning. Looking back on his life, and on the apparent fulfilment in love achieved by others, he could not but be struck by his own isolation. The first *Elegy* therefore took up the promise made in 'Requiem for a Friend' to create an angel out of death, an angel which would rescue her from that oblivion — that unattainability for himself — in which she now had her being. Paula was the prototype of a whole galaxy of women from whom Rilke had sought some word of comfort for himself and for that dead creature in himself whom his mother had loved and dressed as a girl. Women whom he loved became to him 'stars' in his night.

Yet the question his Duino experience raised was 'Who, if I called, would hear me from among the ranks of the angels?' That recall to humility and to his own helplessness meant the breakdown of all previous conceptions of his task, and explains why he had shunned it for so long. Now he knew that if he were to be touched by an angel he would die. For 'beauty is only the beginning of the terrible, and we admire it only because it calmly disdains to destroy us'. Was it possible for the living to do without the dead altogether? Better, like the angels, to make no great distinction between them.

In the second *Elegy* Rilke took up this idea. He represents the world of angels as the world of creative powers, and contrasts it with the vanishing world of man, which abandons even lovers. It opens: 'Every angel is terrible' ('Jeder Engel ist schrecklich'), and asks, who are the angels?

> The early fortunate, creation's favourites,
> mountain ranges, dawn-red ridges
> of all creative things, — pollen of blossoming godhead,
> light articulate, corridors, stairways, thrones,
> spaces of being, shields of delight, tumults
> of stormily-rapturous feeling, and suddenly, singly,
> mirrors, bringing back within their countenance
> the beauty which they radiate.

> Frühe Geglückte, ihr Verwöhnten der Schöpfung,
> Höhenzüge, morgenrötliche Grate
> aller Erschaffung, — Pollen der blühenden Gottheit,
> Gelenke des Lichtes, Gänge, Treppen, Throne,
> Räume aus Wesen, Schilde aus Wonne, Tumulte
> stürmisch entzückten Gefühls und plötzlich, einzeln,
> *Spiegel:* die die entströmte eigene Schönheit
> wiederschöpfen zurück in das eigene Antlitz.

In *The Book of Hours* angels had occurred as aspects of light, rather than as the dark divine power, but Lucifer had sought shelter among them and so for Rilke there was also something satanic about them. In the early versions of the poems they had forgotten how to fly, and how to sing; like the Botticelli angels reproduced by Ruth Mövius in *Rainer Maria Rilkes Stunden-Buch* (1937), they seemed to expect some form of redemption themselves. Rilke wonders in the second *Elegy* whether the angels really caught up like mirrors what was their own, or whether, as if through an oversight, something of ours was retained in them. Death, that 'other side' is thus also a theme, the death he felt himself to be near, as well as close to all lovers. Rilke asks the lovers: 'Have you proofs?' Is he referring to something deeper than human love? Then the proof desired would be whether love is superior to death and conquers it. There was a distinction, he noted, between the act of loving and the lovers themselves.

'Eines ist, die Geliebte zu singen': 'It is one thing to sing of the beloved', but entirely different to accept that 'river-god of the blood', to whom Rilke attributed man's and his own sense of guilt. The third *Elegy* recalls the ancient and elementary power of the blood, and of ancestral tradition. The past is dead except insofar as it lives in us, and in us, only love can control the blood. Rilke feels he would have been unable to withstand the terrors of the blood, or their dark unconscious pleasures, except for his mother who had tucked him in at night and explained away all the frightening shadows and sounds: 'never a rustle you did not explain with a smile' ('Nirgends ein Knistern, das du nicht lächelnd erklärtest'), and yet, eluding her 'behind the cupboard strode / tall in a coat, his fate...' ('hinter den Schrank trat / hoch im Mantel sein Schicksal'). The mother could not, however, cope with the world within, the world the boy loved 'and descended into the older blood as if it were a ravine', where the most horrible thing of all smiled at him as even his mother did not smile.

The forces behind these feelings are cosmic: the poet addresses the stars, asking 'is it not from you that the lover derives his delight in the face of his beloved?' ('Ihr Sterne, / stammt nicht von euch des Liebenden Lust zu dem Antlitz / seiner Geliebten?') He tells the girl: 'You did terrify his heart, but older fears / broke over him at the touching contact.' ('Zwar du erschrakst ihm das Herz; doch ältere Schrecken / stürzten in ihn bei dem berührenden Anstoss.') Human love, he says, is not like that of flowers; ancestors and future generations are implicated in it; from the veins of the youthful lover, 'Dead children wanted to come to you'. He pleads with the girl:

> ... O gently, gently
> Do something for him, a good piece of work, — take him
> close to the garden, give him the full weight
> of night....
>   Preserve him....

> ... O leise, leise,
> tu ein liebes vor ihm, ein verlässliches Tagwerk, — führ ihn
> nah an den Garten heran, gieb ihm der Nächte
> ¨ Ubergewicht....
>   Verhalt ihn....

The personal import of the poem emerges, in this fear of procreation, of his own inner love. While a philosophical approach is legitimate, in that Rilke was attempting an explanation of his place in the universe, it must be said that he had no philosophic pretensions, in the sense of applying his own vision of reality to others. What others might share at most were common experiences, and his conceptions of human life.

In the fourth *Elegy* — 'O Bäume Lebens, o wann winterlich?' — Rilke concluded that the nature of feeling was not known to man, but only what formed it from the outside. We are the playthings of fate, like the dancer Vera Knoop. 'I do not want these half-filled masks, / Rather the doll...' ('Ich will nicht diese halbgefüllten Masken, / lieber die Puppe.') Such a vision of life, as entirely manipulated, was not one to be borne for long. As if his heart were a theatre, Rilke declared he would sit and wait and see what happened. He appealed to his father and all those whom he had loved to say whether or not he was right. In this battle of the heart with the intellect, Rilke remains the observer of all he has loved, until the 'space within your faces became part of the world-space / in which you were no more' ('weil mir der Raum in eurem Angesicht, / da ich ihn liebte, überging in Weltraum, / in dem ihr nicht mehr wart...'). Nothing is itself alone, however, as he had once thought. As he sat and watched his heart, it seemed to him that the Angel again appeared, and that it was all a play. The Angel was required, to 'counterpoise his gaze'.

The lives he saw around him were full of pretexts, and these were inimical to real life. Rilke thought of his childhood, of how the same forces had thwarted him then and ever since; of how they, responsible for the fear he had thought lay in the blood, had in fact murdered his being.

> Murderers are
> easy to understand. But this: to contain death,
> the whole of death, *before* life even, and not be angry,
> is not to be put into words.

> Mörder sind
> leicht einzusehen. Aber dies: den Tod,
> den ganzen Tod, noch *vor* dem Leben so
> sanft zu enthalten und nicht bös zu sein,
> ist unbeschreiblich.

In the fifth *Elegy,* dedicated to Frau Hertha Koenig, in whose Munich flat Rilke sat and watched the Picasso painting, he dealt with the 'Saltimbanques'. These became the symbol of humanity which was still the prey of unknown forces: 'but he wrestles them, / swings them, clings to them and turns them, / throws them and catches them back...' ('Sondern er wringt sie, / biegt sie, schlingt sie und schwingt sie, / wirft sie und fängt sie zurück'). Interrupting these acrobatic images, which display a brilliant technique, comes the second section: 'Ah and around all this / centre the rose of gazing / blossoms and sheds its leaves.' ('Ach und um diese / Mitte, die Rose des Zuschauns: / blüht und entblättert.') Returning to the acrobats, Rilke finds a connection between himself and the young man who goes through the most complicated tricks with tears in his eyes and a smile on his face. Perhaps he was thinking of his own days at the military academy. He asks the Angel to preserve the smile of the boy in a vase as the early emanation of grace, the first component of that cup of which he had once written to Clara, saying that he was gathering herbs for a drink he hoped to prepare for God. Still watching the stage of his heart, Rilke summons up a young girl who endeavours to match her movements to those of the boy, the imperfect worldly achievement of lovers. He addresses the Angel: might there not be somewhere for lovers who had failed on earth, where they might manage to be happy together? The question closes the elegy.

The sixth *Elegy,* one of the most beautiful, opens: 'Feigenbaum, seit wie lange schon ists mir bedeutend...'. The fig-tree was significant for Rilke in the way it began to produce its fruit even before it had properly blossomed. Humans lingering over their flowering were too late in fruiting except for the hero. He rushed ahead into new constellations of danger, wonderfully close to the newly-dead. Rilke too would have liked to escape from his longing in that way. The hero was significant for him only as one who would not allow himself to be held back by love, who 'stormed through all love's resting-places': another Cornet.

It is made plain in the seventh *Elegy* that Rilke could not be of this stamp: he would call out to his love even now, only it would serve no useful purpose. Not a single girl but hundreds would come, all the neglected and misunderstood. He had mentioned Gaspara Stampa, the Italian sonneteer of unrequited love, in the first *Elegy* as a kind of self-reproach, had asked whether old sufferings should not now be more fruitful: 'Is it not time that, loving, / we free ourselves from the beloved and tremblingly withstand the shock...' ('Ist es nicht Zeit, dass wir liebend / uns vom Geliebten befrein und es bebend bestehn...'). The fruitfulness can only be inward. Rilke warns, revealingly: 'Do not think that fate is more than the complex of childhood' ('Glaubt nicht, Schicksal sei mehr, als das Dichte der Kindheit'). The external world is seen to diminish, as in Rilke's letters of the period. He was one of the disinherited, one of those who had lost the love that was rightly theirs and were therefore cut off from human society. Yet, he said, he would reveal what he had seen on earth, the 'form he still recognized', to the angels, so that it should be preserved through eternity by their glance. It is a Shakespearean gesture, 'Not marble, nor the gilded monuments / Of princes, shall outlive this powerful rhyme'. Poetry was to rescue all he had loved, for it was the mission of the poet to transform the whole earth, not simply his own feeling, into the invisible and so give it permanence. This was not to be thought of as an approach to the Angel; his own hand was still raised, warning and warding it off as unattainable. One might consider it a Gnostic concept; Rilke suggested to Hulewicz a similarity 'with the angelic figures of Islam'.

The eighth *Elegy* places man in his environment, between the animals who are unaware of death, and the angels, the forces of creation of whom man knows nothing. It is different in form from the others, with shorter lines, and is dedicated to Rudolf Kassner, with whose ideas it deals to some extent. Rilke portrays the animal world where the concept of death does not exist: 'His being is to him eternal... / Where we see future, it sees everything, / and itself in everything and healed forever.' ('Doch sein Sein ist ihm / unendlich... / Und wo wir Zukunft sehn, dort sieht es Alles / und sich in Allem und geheilt für immer.') Lovers too approach this state, and would be closer to it if they did not too often merely block each other's vision. Man's fate was to observe and watch: 'to be opposite / and nothing else and always opposite' ('gegenüber sein / und nichts als das und immer gegenüber').

The ninth *Elegy* is a call to man to act as an independent, responsible creature. Right action consists in praising what is, in accepting the world as it is, as a valuable part of the whole, given into our hands. For this reason Rilke found himself able to praise life in this elegy, so magnificently, that he was unable to tear himself away from the irrevocable splendour of earthly life, and expressed in ever newer variations what we are and what we have. Why avoid fate and yet long for it? The visible world stood in need of us, and became expressible through us. The fate of the external world thus continually absorbed Rilke, while he knew man to be the most fleeting of creatures. It was a great thing to be on earth: understanding that was man's task. What did we take over into the far country? To whom could we say what we had seen? That was the test and there the intellect broke down.

Those who return from the mountain bring gentians, not a handful of earth. Were we, he asked, here to say, 'House, bridge, well, door...

possibly: pillar, spire?' Perhaps, only better and with more intensity
than they had ever been said before. The poet at least felt that to be one
of his tasks. Having thus made his peace with nature and with the
world, in the tenth *Elegy* Rilke could proclaim his intention to sing the
praise of the visible world to the angels: 'Let me this once at the gates
of grim insight / Praise and glory sing to assenting angels.' ('Das ich
dereinst, an dem Ausgang der grimmigen Einsicht, / Jubel und Ruhm
aufsinge zustimmenden Engeln.')

Afraid of death no longer, Rilke was able to look on death's own
country as he had looked on the deserts of Egypt. This 'Landschaft der
Klagen', Land of Lamentation, was not simply the equivalent of Egypt
but, as it were, a reflection of the Nile in the desert, a clarity of dead
consciousness. Rilke had in fact been burned by contact with the
Angel, as he thought he would be, and could not recover. The haunting
nature of his vision has rarely been equalled. It has a peculiarly personal
significance, it rejects elements of chance and the possibility of
miracles; it is undoubtedly genuine and of cosmic proportions.

The elegies were less a discovery of a new land than a return to the
old, and an attempt to face final reality. Rilke's greatest discovery was
not the angels since they, as much as God, had been isolated from life,
but earth itself seen with new eyes. Even in the days when he wrote
that the 'earth was like a child that knew poems', he had always shared
the Russian love of the soil. In the ninth *Elegy* he asks:

> Earth, is what you want not this: to arise
> *invisibly,* in us? — Is it not your dream
> to become invisible?

> Erde, ist es nicht dies, was du willst: *unsichtbar*
> in uns erstehn? — Ist es dein Traum nicht,
> einmal unsichtbar zu sein?

That is, to become invisible in us. He spoke to the earth as to the
beloved in a marriage ceremony: 'Erde, du liebe, ich will!' 'I will.'

Rilke succeeded in the tenth *Elegy* in using the life we know so well
as a symbol for all that the Angel does not see, and which he passes by
as though it were not there.

> Oh how alien are the streets of Sorrow-City
> where in the false silence stridency creates
> discharged from the moulding-box of vacancy
> the gilded din, the exploding memorial blare.

O how an angel's foot would crush without a trace
their consoling market, flanked by the ready-made church,
clean and closed and disillusioned as a post-office on Sunday.
Outside though, spreading over the edges of the Fair,
swingboats to freedom! Acrobats and conjurors of glee!
And the shooting-range of metaphor and lovely luck
wriggling round the target, and yet like lead
when the skilled hit the mark. Then from applause to chance
he tumbles on, for every curiosity
has a booth to advertise, drum, blubber, though grown-ups
simply must see how money propagates anatomically,
not just for pleasure: the sexual organ of money,
everything, the works, the process, is instructive and
makes fruitful...
.... yet oh just beyond,
behind the last board, covered with posters for 'The Immortal',
that bitter beer that always to the drinker tastes sweet
if he keeps on chewing the cud of fresh distraction...
just behind the plank, at the back, it's all for real.
Children play, and lovers cling to one another, apart,
earnestly in the stricken grass, and dogs cock up a leg.

Freilich, wehe, wie fremd sind die Gassen der Leid-Stadt,
wo in der falschen, aus Übertönung gemachten
Stille, stark, aus der Gussform des Leeren der Ausguss
prahlt der vergoldete Lärm, das platzende Denkmal.
O, wie spürlos zerträte ein Engel ihnen den Trostmarkt,
den die Kirche begrenzt, ihre fertig gekaufte:
reinlich und zu und enttäuscht wie ein Postamt am Sonntag.
Draussen aber kräuseln sich immer die Ränder von Jahrmarkt.
Schaukeln der Freiheit! Taucher und Gaukler des Eifers!
Und des behübschten Glücks figürliche Schiessstatt,
wo es zappelt von Ziel und sich blechern benimmt,
wenn ein Geschickterer trifft. Von Beifall zu Zufall
täumelt er weiter; denn Buden jeglicher Neugier
werben, trommeln und plärrn. Für Erwachsene aber
ist noch besonders zu sehn, wie das Geld sich vermehrt,
                                        anatomisch,
nicht zur Belustigung nur: der Geschlechtsteil des Gelds,

alles, das Ganze, der Vorgang —, das unterrichtet und macht
fruchtbar . . .
. . . Oh aber gleich darüber hinaus,
hinter der letzten Planke, beklebt mit Plakaten des 'Todlos',
jenes bitteren Biers, das den Trinkenden süss scheint,
wenn sie immer dazu frische Zerstreuungen kaun . . . ,
gleich im Rücken der Planke, gleich dahinter, ists *wirklich.*
Kinder spielen, und Liebende halten einander, — abseits,
ernst, im ärmlichen Gras, und Hunde haben Natur.

It was nothing but a world of substitutes. A flaunting world of
advertisements held out the promise of immortality in beer. Stalls and
shops offered distractions and sops of every kind to frightened egotism.
Institutions had become a compound of fear, greed and superstition.
'Nature' was a synonym for 'dirty'.

The mountains around, mountains of grief, were the home of the
creative spirit and all that man denied. There girls belonged to the race
of Lamentations, for that high world contained everything that was
rejected in towns: ruined castles, trees blossoming tears; fields not of
flax but of melancholy; and the significant constellations of childhood:
the 'Rider', 'Cradle', 'M' for mothers. The poet was home.

The task of the dead was to learn the meaning of primeval suffering:
'Lonely he advances into the mountains of original suffering. / And
not even his footsteps resound from that silent fate.' ('Einsam steigt er
dahin, in die Berge des Ur-Leids. / Und nicht einmal sein Schritt klingt
aus dem tonlosen Los.') Rilke believed that until death we have the
strength to transform the world inside ourselves, our inner space being
wider and greater than external space. As we are filled in life with the
world and with everyone, including the dead of the earth, so after
death we may live within later human beings. Inner psychological
space, to Rilke, was an imaginary space which offered infinite
possibilities of living intensely at the very heart of life.

Here Rilke came near to Goethe's view of the persistence of all life
that attains completeness. In 1813 Goethe, in a conversation after the
death of Wieland, described his conception of limited immortality:

As for the personal persistence of our spirit after death, I see it as
follows. It is in no way contradictory to the observation I have been
making for many years of the nature of all creatures, but can on the
contrary actually be given new proof from these. That such high
forces in nature should perish is out of the question entirely. Nature

is never so extravagant with her capital. There is no possibility at all
of annihilation.

At the end of the last *Elegy,* as a clue to the nature of death, Rilke offers
the symbol of the downward-hanging catkin and the falling rain: we
who are used to thinking of rising joy are asked to conceive of it as
falling, perhaps like the shooting-star he had once seen from a bridge in
Toledo.

If the *Elegies* are an abandonment of the mythological approach in
favour of 'reality', even a kind of super-reality, the *Sonnets to Orpheus*
are the mythological expression of emotion. In them Rilke sought not
to free himself from the burden of love, but like Orpheus, to trace his
Eurydice lost in the depths of the earth. The dualism we have noted in
Rilke from his earliest years is contained in these two attitudes, the
search for the stars and for the earth. Valéry's 'Cimetière Marin'
includes a fine passage on biological metamorphosis, which no doubt
influenced Rilke deeply, though it displayed an attitude to which he
was already prone. He had affinities too with the Orphic doctrines: the
dualism between soul and body, which he had striven to reject; the
doctrine of reincarnation, common to most great Eastern religions;
and the idea of magical transformation.

In the first sonnet Rilke invokes the Tree of Sound, Orpheus's song,
and in so doing, his own power of music. By the force of music Rilke
creates the form of a young girl, who sleeps within the poet's ear and
dreams of life and of the world. Vera had already occurred as the
'dancer' in the *Elegies,* now she — and possibly Benvenuta — occurs
again in the form of music, but the sleeping girl who would not waken
was the girl of Rilke's dreams. All poets are identified with Orpheus,
whose song is sheer enchantment (Sonnet IX):

> Only he who has raised the lyre
> even under shadow
> dare divine and return
> unending praise.
>
> Only he who has eaten the poppy seed
> with the dead
> will capture the
> slightest sound.

> Nur wer die Leier schon hob
> auch unter Schatten,
> darf das unendliche Lob
> ahnend erstatten.
>
> Nur wer mit Toten vom Mohn
> ass, von dem ihren,
> wird nicht den leisesten Ton
> wieder verlieren.

Who then was Orpheus, he asks in Sonnet VI, as he had asked of the angels. 'Ist er ein Hiesiger?'

> Does he belong here? No, in both
> kingdoms his nature grew.
> The branches of the willows
> are parted better by those who know the roots.
>
> Ist er ein Hiesiger? Nein, aus beiden
> Reichen erwuchs seine weite Natur.
> Kundiger böge die Zweige der Weiden,
> wer die Wurzeln der Weiden erfuhr.

Orpheus had eaten poppy-seeds with the dead and could wander at will between their kingdom and that of the living: there is no clear line of demarcation. Even the glories of the ancient world come to the surface and are used for quite other purposes: men ploughing in the tombs; ancient sarcophagi used as troughs; one life passed into another. The process of change is seen to be unceasing, whether in the growth of plants or the transmigration of souls. The solid fruits of the earth themselves belonged to both life and death.

> The round apple, pear, banana,
> gooseberry... all these speak
> death and life in the mouth... I feel...
> Read it on a child's face
>
> when it tastes them. That comes from afar.
> Slowly becomes nameless, in the mouth?
> Where words were, treasures flow
> freed from the flesh of the fruit.

Dare to say what you call apple.
That sweetness which, intense,
slowly dissolves in taste

to become clear and transparent,
ambiguous, sunny, earthy, here
belonging, o experience, feeling, joy unlimited!

Voller Apfel, Birne und Banane,
Stachelbeere... Alles dieses spricht
Tod und Leben in den Mund... Ich ahne...
Lese es einem Kind vom Angesicht,

wenn es sie erschmeckt. Dies kommt von weit.
Wird euch langsam namenlos im Munde?
Wo sonst Worte waren, fliessen Funde,
aus dem Fruchtfleisch überrascht befreit.

Wagt zu sagen, was ihr Apfel nennt.
Diese Süsse, die sich erst verdichtet,
um, im Schmecken leise aufgerichtet,

klar zu werden, wach und transparent,
doppeldeutig, sonnig, erdig, hiesig —:
O Erfahrung, Fühlung, Freude —, riesig!

                              Sonnet XIII

The whole of the first part of the sonnets deals with the various
forms of metamorphosis: the musical and aesthetic; the emotional and
spiritual; the biological, the evolutionary; the seasonal and historical;
almost as if Rilke were trying to seize the fleeting nature of life itself
and incorporate it into the form of Orpheus.

> The world changes swift
> as the shapes of cloud,
> all that is complete
> falls home.

Over change and progress,
further and freer,
lending us your old song,
God with the lyre.

Sorrows are not known,
love is not learnt,
and what removes us in death

is not discovered.
Only song over all
blesses and praises.

Wandelt sich rasch auch die Welt
wie Wolkengestalten,
alles Vollendete fällt
heim zum Uralten.

Uber dem Wandel und Gang,
weiterund freier,
währt noch dein Vor-Gesang,
Gott mit der Leier.

Nicht sind die Leiden erkannt,
nicht ist die Liebe gelernt,
und was im Tod uns entfernt,

ist nicht entschleiert.
Einzig das Lied überm Land
heiligt und feiert.

Sonnet XIX

Rilke finds himself capable of metamorphoses, of identifications where
the components are inseparable, as in the opening sonnet in the second
section; 'Breathing, you invisible poem!' ('Atmen, du unsichtbares
Gedicht!'):

Do you know me air, once full of my places?
You, once the smooth rind,
Rounding and leaf of my words.

Erkennst du mich, Luft, du, voll noch einst meiniger Orte?
Du, einmal glatte Rinde,
Rundung und Blatt meiner Worte.

In opposition to this kind of organic identification stood the
relationship between man and machine, against which Rilke gently
warned in the lovely twenty-second sonnet:

> Young men do not throw your courage
> into the love of speed
> or attempts at flight.
>
> All is at rest:
> darkness and light,
> flower and book.
>
> Knaben, o werft den Mut
> nicht in die Schnelligkeit,
> nicht in den Flugversuch.
>
> Alles ist ausgeruht:
> Dunkel und Helligkeit,
> Blume und Buch.

From the world of things, passivity and real power, which was the
power of the potential, could be learned. The danger of the machine
was that it threatened everything man had acquired because it insisted
on trying to penetrate the world of the spirit, instead of being content
to obey (see section II, sonnet XI). It lent itself too easily to man's spirit
of restlessness and avoidance of inner spiritual conflict. More than that,
it infected men with its restricted, mechanical reaction, as previous
civilizations built on slavery had been infected by that.

To the end, Rilke maintained that the essence of nature was balance
and rest and proportion — as indeed it was of art — and that sooner or
later the natural world would revenge itself on man for his frightful
pillaging. But his expression of this conviction is couched in subjective
terms, as in sonnet XXVII (section II):

Giebt es wirklich die Zeit, die zerstörende?
Wann, auf dem ruhenden Berg, zerbricht sie die Burg?
Dieses Herz, das unendlich den Göttern gehörende,
wann vergewaltigts der Demiurg?

Sind wir wirklich so ängstlich Zerbrechliche,
wie das Schicksal uns wahr machen will?
Ist die Kindheit, die tiefe, versprechliche,
in den Wurzeln — später — still?

'Does time as a destructive factor really exist?' he asks in this poem. If
so, at what precise moment does it destroy the castle on the hill? When
will the demi-urge destroy the heart that belongs to the gods? Are we
really so fearfully fragile as fate seems to indicate? Is childhood, which
promises so much, one day still, down to the very roots? He concludes
that as the manifestation of permanent forces, men, transitory as they
are individually, have a validity as 'divine custom' ('göttlicher
Brauch'). This same sense of our actions having an immortal
significance occurs in sonnet XXIV (second section):

Gods, we plan them in bold relief
and sullen fate destroys our plans.
But they are the immortals.

Götter, wir planen sie erst in erkühnten Entwürfen,
die uns das mürrische Schicksal wieder zerstört.
Aber sie sind die Unsterblichen.

This should be set alongside his letter to Ilse Blumenthal-Weiss from
Muzot (28 December 1921):

Faith! There is no such thing, I had almost said. There is only
— Love. This forcing of the heart to regard this and that as
true, which is ordinarily called Faith, has no sense. First one
must find God somewhere, experience Him as so infinite, so
great, so incredibly present that whether it is fear, or
astonishment, or breathlessness, or finally love that one feels for
Him matters little, — but belief, that effort towards God, has
no place when one has begun to discover God, for there is then
no stopping, no matter where one began.

Faith can be given to many things that are not God, many things even
opposed to God; it is not easy to deceive love. Faith is often bound up
with a powerful sense of self which may be lost in love: such a
destruction of the 'I' increased in importance for Rilke. Concentration
on the material, the 'thing', was what he was learning as he wrote the
New Poems, but in that collection he presents in 'Liebes-Lied' ('Love
Song') conflicting kinds of self-forgetfulness:

> How shall I withhold my soul
> from touching yours? How shall I
> raise it above you to other things?
> Gladly would I hide it
> somewhere in the dark among the lost
> in some quiet, strange spot, that will not vibrate
> when your depths vibrate.
> But all that touches us, unites us
> together like a bow-stroke
> drawing a voice from two strings.
> On what instrument are we strung?
> What player holds us in his hand?
> O sweet song!

> Wie soll ich meine Seele halten, dass
> sie nicht an deine rührt? Wie soll ich sie
> hinheben über dich zu andern Dingen?
> Ach gerne möcht ich sie bei irgendwas
> Verlorenem im Dunkel unterbringen
> an einer fremden stillen Stelle, die
> nicht weiterschwingt, wenn deine Tiefen schwingen.
> Doch alles, was uns anrührt, dich und mich,
> nimmt uns zusammen wie ein Bogenstrich,
> der aus zwei Seiten *eine* stimme zieht.
> Auf welches Instrument sind wir gespannt?
> Und welcher Geiger hat uns in der Hand?
> O süsses Lied.

Whenever real love streamed out from the reality of one individual to
that of another there occurred a rare pause, Rilke thought, when life as
it were drew breath; a brief instant when everything coalesced into a
deep calm; one in which separation had been bridged and everything
returned to its source. The deeper reality of lovers taught one to look

away from oneself, and understand that an individual was nothing in
and for himself. It was the surrender of the self, the sacrifice of what
was personal, that could lead to awareness of the deepest level of
existence. Every individual, at least once in his life, knows an hour or
perhaps only a minute, of having his 'veins full of being', as Rilke said.
This dissolution of the self in love constitutes for Rilke the process by
which we share in the infinite nature of being, allows us to feel that we
fit into the design of the world. He describes this potential release from
self-consciousness in a poem inscribed in a copy of his early works for
Frau Wunderly, dated 31 January 1922:

> As long as you catch what you threw, everything
> is skill and calculable profit —;
> only when you suddenly catch the ball
> thrown to you by a fellow-player
> constantly, to your centre, in a practised
> expert swing, in one of those arcs
> of God's great bridge constructions:
> only then is skill in catching real ability,
> not yours, a world's. And if you should
> possess the strength and courage to throw back,
> no, more miraculous still: strength and courage forget —
> and already have thrown... (as the year
> casts forth the birds, the migrant swarms
> overseas propelled by an older to a newer warmth)
> only then in that venture are you really in the game.
> No longer make it easy for yourself to throw:
> nor make it harder. Out of your hand slips
> the meteor and races to its spaces.

> Solang due Selbstgeworfnes fängst, ist alles
> Geschicklichkeit und lässlicher Gewinn —;
> erst wenn du plötzlich Fänger wirst des Balles,
> den eine ewige Mit-Spielerin
> dir zuwarf, deiner Mitte, in genau
> gekonntem Schwung, in einem jener Bogen
> aus Gottes grossem Brücken-Bau:
> erst dann ist Fangen-Können ein Vermögen, —
> nicht deines, einer Welt. Und wenn du gar
> zurückzuwerfen Kraft und Mut besässest

nein, wunderbarer: Mut und Kraft vergässest
und schon geworfen *hättest*... (wie das Jahr
die Vögel wirft, die Wandervogelschwärme,
die eine ältre einer jungen Wärme
hinüberschleudert über Meere —) erst
in diesem Wagnis spielst du gültig mit.
Erleichterst dir den Wurf nicht mehr; erschwerst
dir ihn nicht mehr. Aus deinen Händen tritt
das Meteor und rast in seine Räume...

Alongside these joyous possibilities exist realities on which Rilke always insisted: pain, suffering, loneliness, relinquishment. 'Lieben heisst allein sein,' he concludes: 'loving means to be alone'. Out of bitter personal experience he constructed such generalizations and made them poetically fruitful. He felt himself 'exposed on the mountains of the heart' ('ausgesetzt auf den Bergen des Herzens'), whence he could see in the land of sorrow 'die letzte Ortschaft der Worte', words, his last village; that is to say poetry, 'ein letztes Gehöft von Gefühl', a last farm of feeling.

In death, he believed, the limitations and restrictions on the individual are finally lifted. Rilke was able to describe death in the ninth *Elegy* as friendly ('der vertrauliche Tod'), but he feared it terribly. What he wrote of Tolstoy in his essay 'On God', however, might be applied to Rilke himself:

This man has observed many forms of the fear of death, in himself and in others, for he could observe his own fear owing to his natural self-command, and his relationship to death was, to the last, a great permeation of fear, a fugue of fear as it were, a gigantic construction, a tower of fear with corridors and stairs and unrailed crags and precipices on all sides — only the strength with which he learned and accepted the display of his fear suddenly changed at the last moment into inaccessible reality, and became the foundation for this tower, and landscape and Heaven, and the wind and the flight of birds.

Rilke was a European wanderer, travelling restlessly without a country, taking and adapting what suited him. Valéry remarked of Rilke that he 'gradually and imperceptibly became a citizen of intellectual Europe. There was a strong affinity between this great poet... and the Slav race. He was an authority on Scandinavia, and so close to French art that I found it easy to tempt him to write poems in French . . .'. And Maurice Betz has written: 'Rilke's journeys were for Europe. The spiritual plains of the globe were for him Russia, Denmark and France. Germany, Austria and Italy came after these.'

For him there was only Europe. The few attempts he made to extend his travels to North Africa and Egypt ended in physical or spiritual defeat. In Rilke's eyes America was the superlative form of one kind of human existence, but it meant to him an 'absolute void'.

It is absolutely my own fault that I have no real home. My family, perhaps, if it had preserved the old home in the part of the country long known to it, might have enabled me to develop a native feeling I could have used in the place I had inherited. The town in which I grew up offered no real foundation for this. Its air was neither the air I breathed, nor the air I lived. Thus it was inevitable that I should choose my homes according to what they promised me, that is, what I involuntarily invented, a kind of kinship wherever I found the visible world picturesque enough to answer the need of my instincts for expression. As long as the world was open to me, and the choice of such a composite home unlimited, everything I acquired became a kind of hovering, and yet sufficiently sustaining, support, extended as it were *across* the various countries.

He had at first been homeless because his parents had not given him a home, later because he had not been able to found one. Rilke had constantly tried to overcome the feeling of isolation in part due to his rootlessness by establishing what he conceived to be a more organic relation with society, and at a deeper level with universal forces. This was the mystic who wrote in his diary for Lou Andreas-Salomé:

Later he thought of certain moments when strength seemed to be contained in them as in a seed. He thought of the time in that southern garden, when the call of a bird outside coincided with his inmost feeling, since it did not seem to break at the frontiers of his body, but to enter and form both worlds into one space, in which, secretly protected, there remained only one single spot, of the clearest, deepest consciousness. Then he closed his eyes, so as not to be confused by the shape of his body, and the infinite entered on all sides, so familiarly, that he thought he felt the stars in his breast.

Everything for Rilke was enclosed in the unity of life, even the forces that lead us out of it: love and death. Our fear is created by what we see as the finality and singleness of death. But in love and death we must, he thought, surrender ourselves completely and become a twin being, or all beings. In love and in death we enter the general life, are given the power of decision and called upon to use it.

> Erect no stone in memory. Let the rose
> blossom every year to his renown.

> Errichtet keinen Denkstein. Lasst die Rose
> nur jedes Jahr zu seinen Gunsten blühen.

Select bibliography

The standard edition of Rilke's works was published in six volumes by the Insel-Verlag in 1927. This edition, revised and edited by Ernst Zinn, republished 1955-66, is generally referred to as *Sämtliche Werke* (SW) I-VI. *Archival holdings:* Weimar Archives at Westerwede bei Bremen; Swiss Archives at Landesbibliothek, Berne; Rilke holdings at the Schiller National Museum, Marbach, Germany; the Richard von Mises Collection, Houghton Library, Harvard University, of which the catalogue is an important bibliography.

Also noteworthy: the Sagan Collection, University of Kansas; the 'Rilke-Bibliographie', published by Walter Ritzler, Vienna, 1951.

Works

SW III	*Leben und Lieder.* Strasburg, Leipzig: Kattentidt, 1894
	Wegwarten. Prague: Selbstverlag des Verfassers, 1895
SW I	*Larenopfer.* Prague: Dominicus, 1896
	Im Frühfrost. Berlin: A. Entsch, 1897
SW I	*Traumgekrönt.* Leipzig: Friesenhahn, 1897
SW I	*Advent.* Leipzig: Friesenhahn, 1898
SW IV	*Am Leben Hin.* Stuttgart: Bonz, 1898
SW IV	*Zwei Prager Geschichten.* Stuttgart: Bonz, 1898
SW III	*Mir Zur Feier.* Berlin: G.H. Meyer, 1899
	Von Lieben Gott und Anderes. Leipzig, 1900
SW IV	*Geschichten vom lieben Gott* (2nd ed). Leipzig, 1904
SW IV	*Die Letzten.* Berlin: Axel Juncker Verlag, 1902
SW I	*Das Buch der Bilder.* Berlin: Axel Juncker Verlag, 1902; 2nd ed. 1906
	Das tägliche Leben. Munich: Albert Langen, 1902
SW V	*Worpswede.* Bielefeld, Leipzig: Velhagen & Klasing, 1903
SW V	*Auguste Rodin.* Berlin: Bard, 1903; 2nd ed. 1907
SW I	*Das Stunden-Buch.* Leipzig: Insel-Verlag, 1905
SW I	*Die Weise von Liebe und Tod des Cornets Christoph Rilke.* Berlin: Axel Juncker Verlag, 1906
SW I	*Neue Gedichte.* Leipzig: Insel-Verlag — publisher henceforth — 1907

SW I   *Der neuen Gedichte anderer Teil.* 1908
SW I   *Requiem.* 1909
SW I   *Die Frühen Gedichte.* 1909
SW V   *Die Aufzeichnungen des Malte Laurids Brigge.* 1910
SW I   *Das Marien-Leben.* 1913
SW I   *Duineser Elegien.* 1923
SW I   *Sonette an Orpheus.* 1923
SW II *Vergers: suivis des quatrains valaisans.* Paris: Editions de la Nouvelle Revue Française, 1926
       Ewald Tragy. Munich: B. Heller, 1929

Translations

The Hogarth Press, London, has published Rilke's major poetry, mostly in translations by J.B. Leishman:

Duino Elegies: with Stephen Spender; 1948
New Poems. 1964
Poems 1906-1926. 1978
Poems from the Book of Hours: tr. A.L. Peck; 1961
Requiem and other poems. 1935
Selected Works: vol II - Poetry. 1960
Sonnets to Orpheus. 1936

An Unofficial Rilke: poems 1912-1926: tr. Michael Hamburger; London, 1981
Life of the Virgin Mary: tr. Stephen Spender; London, 1971

Ewald Tragy: tr. Lola Gruenthal; London, 1958
Rodin: trs. Jessie Lamont and Hans Trausil; London, 1946
Stories of God: tr. William Rose; London, 1932
The Notebooks of Malte Laurids Brigge: tr. John Linton, London, 1930

Letters

The Insel-Verlag published 5 volumes in the series *Briefe und Tagebücher aus den Jahren: 1899-1902* (1931); *1902-1906* (1930); *1906-1907* (1930); *1907-1914* (1933); *1914-1921* (1937). A further 5 volumes: *Gesammelte Briefe 1892-1926* (1939–40). Other correspondence published by Insel-Verlag:
Briefe an seinen Verleger 1906-1926. 2 vols, 2nd ed. 1949
Briefe aus Muzot 1921-1926. 1935
Briefe an Auguste Rodin. 1928

Briefe an einen jungen Dichter. 1929
Briefe über Cézanne. 1952
Briefe an Frau Gudi Nölke. 1953
Briefwechsel R.M. Rilke und Lou Andreas-Salomé. 1952
Briefwechsel R.M. Rilke – Maria von Thurn und Taxis Hohenloe. 1958
Briefwechsel R.M. Rilke und Katharina Kippenberg. 1954
Briefwechsel in Gedichten mit Erika Mitterer. 1950
Briefwechsel mit Benvenuta. Esslingen, 1954
R.M. Rilke – André Gide, Correspondance. Paris, 1952
Lettres milanaises, 1921-1926 Paris, 1956
R.M. Rilke et Merline: Correspondance 1920-1926. Zurich, 1954

Translations

Correspondence in Verse with Erika Mitterer: tr. N.K. Cruickshank;
    London, 1953
Letters 1892-1910, 1910-1926: trs. J.B. Greene and M.D. Herter Norton; New
    York, 1972
Letters of R.M. Rilke and Princess Marie von Thurn und Taxis: tr. Nora
    Wydenbruck; London, 1958
Letters to a Young Poet: tr. Reginald Snell; London, 1945
Letters to Benvenuta: tr. Heinz Norden; London
Letters to Frau Gudi Nölke: tr. Violet MacDonald; London, 1965
Letters to Merline: tr. Violet MacDonald; London, 1951
Selected Letters of R.M. Rilke 1902-1926: tr. R.F.C. Hull; London, 1946
Unpublished Letters to Mrs Eloui Bey: tr. W.B. Kennedy; New York, 1952

Secondary Works

Albert-Lasard, Lou: *Wege mit Rilke.* Frankfurt, 1952
Andreas-Salomé, Lou: *Rainer Maria Rilke.* Leipzig, 1929
Baer, Lydia: 'Rilke and J.P. Jacobsen', *PMLA* 54 (1939), pp. 100–32,
    1133–1180
Barron, Frank (ed.): *Rilke: the alchemy of alienation.* Lawrence, Kansas,
    1980
Basserman, Dieter: *Der späte Rilke.* Munich, 1947
Basserman, Dieter: *Der andere Rilke.* Bad Homburg, 1961
Batterby, K.A.J.: *Rilke and France.* Oxford, 1966
Bauer, Arnold: *Rainer Maria Rilke.* Berlin, 1970 (tr. Ursula Lamm, New
    York, 1972)
Betz, Maurice: *Rilke à Paris.* Paris, 1941
Betz, Maurice: *Rilke vivant.* Paris, 1937

Bianquis, Geneviève: *La poésie autrichienne de Hofmannsthal à Rilke.* Paris, 1926

Buddeberg, Elsie: *R.M. Rilke: eine innerer Biographie.* Stuttgart, 1955

Butler, E.M.: *Rainer Maria Rilke.* Cambridge, 1941

Casey, Timothy: *R.M. Rilke: a centenary essay.* London, 1976

Cox, Richard: *Figures of Transformation: Rilke and the example of Valéry.* London, 1979

Dehn, Fritz: *R.M. Rilke und sein Werk.* Leipzig, 1934

Demetz, Peter: *René Rilkes Prager Jahre.* Düsseldorf, 1953

Fuerst, Norbert: *Phases of Rilke.* Indiana, 1958

Gebser, Hans: *Rilke und Spanien.* Zurich, 1940

Goldsmith, Ulrich K.: *R.M. Rilke: a verse concordance to his complete lyric poetry.* Leeds, 1980

Graff, Willem Laurens: *Rainer Maria Rilke.* Princeton, 1956

Guardini, Romano: *Rilke's Duino Elegies.* London, 1961

Hattingberg, Magda von: *Rilke und Benvenuta.* Vienna, 1943

Heerikhuizen, F.W. van: *R.M. Rilke: his life and work.* London, 1952

Hell, Victor: *Rainer Maria Rilke.* Paris, 1965

Holthausen, Hans-Egon: *R.M. Rilke: a study of his later poetry.* Cambridge, 1952

Jaloux, Edmond: *Rainer Maria Rilke.* Paris, 1927

Klatt, Fritz: *Sieg uber die Angst.* Berlin, 1940

Koenig, Herta: *Rilkes Mutter.* Pfüllingen/Tubingen, 1963

Mandel, Siegfried: *R.M. Rilke: the poetic instinct.* Illinois, 1965

Mason, Eudo C.: *Rilke's Apotheosis.* Oxford, 1938

Mason, Eudo C.: *Rilke, Europe and the English-Speaking World.* Cambridge, 1961

Mason, Eudo C.: *Rilke.* Edinburgh, 1963

Mayer, Gerhart: *Rilke und Kassner.* Bonn, 1960

Modersohn-Becker, Paula: *Briefe und Tagebuchblatter.* Linz, 1920

Mörchen, Hermann: *Rilkes Sonette an Orpheus.* Stuttgart, 1958

Mövius, Ruth: *R.M. Rilkes Stunden-Buch.* Leipzig, 1937

Musil, Robert: *Rede zur Rilke Feier, 16 Jan.* Berlin, 1927

Nevar, Elya Maria: *Freundschaft mit R.M. Rilke.* Berne, 1946

Perry, Gillian: *Paula Modersohn-Becker.* London, 1979

Peters, Heinz Friedrich: *Masks and the Man.* Seattle, 1960

Quiel, Friedrich: *Rilkes Vermächtnis.* Bodman/Bodensee, 1972

Rilke, Phia: *Ephemeriden.* Graz, 1947

Rolleston, James: *Rilke in Transition.* New Haven, 1970

Rose, W. and Craig-Houston, C. (eds): *R.M. Rilke: aspects of his mind and poetry.* London, 1938

Saalman, Dieter: *R.M. Rilkes Die Aufzeichnungen.* Bonn, 1975

Salis, J.R. von: *R.M. Rilkes Schweizer Jahre.* Leipzig, 1938 (tr. N.K. Cruickshank, London, 1964)

Schlözer, Leopold von: *R.M. Rilke on Capri*. Dresden, 1931

Schmidt-Pauli, Elizabeth: *R.M. Rilke: ein Gedenkbuch*. Basel, 1940

Schnack, Ingeborg: *Leben und Werk im Bild*. Frankfurt, 1973

Schoolfield, George: *Rilke's Last Year*. Kansas, 1969

Sieber, Carl: *René Rilke: Die Jugend Rainer Maria Rilkes*. Leipzig, 1932

Solbrig, Ingeborg and Storck, Joachim: *Rilke Heute* (2 vols). Frankfurt, 1975, 1976

Stahl, E.H. (ed.): *Rilke's Duineser Elegien*. Oxford, 1965

Steiner, Jacob: *Rilkes Duineser Elegien*. Berlin, 1962

Stephen, Anthony: *R.M. Rilke's Gedichte an die Nacht*. Cambridge, 1972

Thurn und Taxis, Princess Marie: *Erinnerungen an R.M. Rilke*. Berlin, 1933

Valéry, Paul et al: *Reconnaissance pour Rilke*. Paris, 1926

Webb, Karl Eugene: *Rainer Maria Rilke*. North Carolina, 1978

Weigand, Elsie: 'Rilke and Eliot', *Germanic Review* 30 (1955), pp. 198-210

Wood, Frank: *R.M. Rilke: the ring of forms*. Minnesota, 1958

Wydenbruck, Nora: *Rilke: man and poet*. London, 1949

Index